KNOW YOUR GOVERNMENT

THE
Democratic Party

KNOW YOUR GOVERNMENT

THE
Democratic
Party

By Justine Rubinstein

MASON CREST
PHILADELPHIA • MIAMI

Mason Crest
450 Parkway Drive, Suite D
Broomall, Pennsylvania 19008
(866) MCP-BOOK (toll-free)
www.masoncrest.com

Printed in the United States of America
First printing
9 8 7 6 5 4 3 2 1

Series ISBN: 978-1-4222-4231-5
Hardcover ISBN: 978-1-4222-4233-9

Cataloging-in-Publication Data is available on file at the Library of Congress.

Developed and Produced by Print Matters Productions, Inc. (www.printmattersinc.com)
Cover and Interior Design by Lori S. Malkin Design, LLC

QR CODES AND LINKS TO THIRD-PARTY CONTENT:

CONTENTS

Key Icons to Look For

Words to Understand: These words with their easy-to-understand definitions will increase readers' understanding of the text while building vocabulary skills.

Sidebars: This boxed material within the main text allows readers to build knowledge, gain insights, explore possibilities, and broaden their perspectives by weaving together additional information to provide realistic and holistic perspectives.

Educational Videos: Readers can view videos by scanning our QR codes, providing them with additional educational content to supplement the text.

Text-Dependent Questions: These questions send the reader back to the text for more careful attention to the evidence presented there.

Research Projects: Readers are pointed toward areas of further inquiry connected to each chapter. Suggestions are provided for projects that encourage deeper research and analysis.

Series Glossary of Key Terms: This back-of-the-book glossary contains terminology used throughout this series. Words found here increase the reader's ability to read and comprehend higher-level books and articles in this field.

The Evolving American Experiment

From the start, Americans have regarded their government with a mixture of reliance and mistrust. The men who founded the republic did not doubt the indispensability of government. "If men were angels," observed the 51st *Federalist Paper*, "no government would be necessary." But men are not angels. Because human beings are subject to wicked as well as to noble impulses, government was deemed essential to ensure freedom and order.

At the same time, the American revolutionaries knew that government could also become a source of injury and oppression. The men who gathered in Philadelphia in 1787 to write the Constitution therefore had two purposes in mind. They wanted to establish a strong central authority and to limit that central authority's capacity to abuse its power.

To prevent the abuse of power, the Founding Fathers wrote two basic principles into the new Constitution. The principle of federalism divided power between the state governments and the central authority. The principle of the separation of powers subdivided the central authority itself into three branches—the executive, the legislative, and the judiciary—so that "each may be a check on the other."

The Constitution did not plan the executive branch in any detail. After vesting the executive power in the president, it assumed the existence of "executive departments" without specifying what these departments should be. Congress began defining their functions in 1789 by creating the Departments of State, Treasury, and War. The secretaries in charge of these departments made up President Washington's first cabinet. Congress also provided for a legal officer, and President Washington soon invited the attorney general, as he was called, to attend cabinet meetings. As need required, Congress created more executive departments.

Setting up the cabinet was only the first step in organizing the American state. With almost no guidance from the Constitution, President Washington, seconded by Alexander Hamilton, his brilliant secretary of the treasury, equipped the infant republic with a working administrative structure. The Federalists believed in both executive energy and executive accountability and set high standards for public appointments. The Jeffersonian opposition had less faith in strong government and preferred local government to the central authority. But when Jefferson himself became president in 1801, although he set out to change the direction of policy, he found no reason to alter the framework the Federalists had erected.

By 1801, there were about 3,000 federal civilian employees in a nation of a little more than 5 million people. Growth in territory and population steadily enlarged national responsibilities. Thirty years later, when Jackson was president, there were more than 11,000 government workers in a nation of 13 million. The federal establishment was increasing at a rate faster than the population.

The United States Constitution has been the supreme law of the United States since its signing in 1787. Its first three words, "We the People," affirm that the government is here to serve the people.

Jackson's presidency brought significant changes in the federal service. Jackson believed that the executive branch contained too many officials who saw their jobs as "species of property" and as "a means of promoting individual interest." Against the idea of a permanent service based on life tenure, Jackson argued for the periodic redistribution of federal offices, contending that this was the democratic way and that official duties could be made "so plain and simple that men of intelligence may readily qualify themselves for their performance." He called this policy *rotation-in-office*. His opponents called it the *spoils system*.

In fact, partisan legend exaggerated the extent of Jackson's removals. More than 80 percent of federal officeholders retained their jobs. Jackson discharged no larger a proportion of government workers than Jefferson had done a generation earlier. But the rise in these years of mass political parties gave federal patronage new importance as a means of building the party and of rewarding activists. Jackson's successors were less restrained in the distribution of spoils. As the federal establishment grew—to nearly 40,000 by 1861—the politicization of the public service excited increasing concern.

After the Civil War, the spoils system became a major political issue. High-minded men condemned it as the root of all political evil. The spoilsmen, said the British commentator James Bryce, "have distorted and depraved the mechanism of politics." Patronage—giving jobs to unqualified, incompetent, and dishonest persons—lowered the standards of public service and nourished corrupt political machines. Office-seekers pursued presidents and cabinet secretaries without mercy. "Patronage," said Ulysses S. Grant after his presidency, "is the bane of the presidential office." "Every time I appoint someone to office," said another political leader, "I make a hundred enemies and one ingrate." George William Curtis, the president of the National Civil Service Reform League, summed up the indictment:

> The theory which perverts public trusts into party spoils, making public employment dependent upon personal favor and not on proved merit, necessarily ruins the self-respect of public employees, destroys the function of party in a republic, prostitutes elections into a desperate strife for personal profit, and degrades the national character by lowering the moral tone and standard of the country.

The object of civil service reform was to promote efficiency and honesty in the public service and to bring about the ethical regeneration of public life. In 1883, over bitter opposition from politicians, the reformers passed the Pendleton Act, establishing a bipartisan Civil Service Commission, competitive examinations, and appointment on merit. The Pendleton Act also gave the president authority to extend by executive order the number of "classified" jobs—that is, jobs subject to the merit system. The act applied initially only to about 14,000 of the more than 100,000 federal positions. But by the end of the nineteenth century, 40 percent of federal jobs had moved into the classified category.

The twentieth century saw a considerable expansion of the federal establishment. The Great Depression and the New Deal led the national government to take on a variety of new responsibilities. The New Deal extended the federal regulatory apparatus. By 1940, in a nation of 130 million people, the number of federal workers for the first time passed the 1 million mark. The Second World War brought federal civilian employment to 3.8 million in 1945. With peace, the federal establishment declined to around 2 million by 1950. Then growth resumed, reaching 2.8 million by the 1980s. In 2017, there were only 2.1 million federal civilian employees.

The New Deal years saw rising criticism of "big government" and "bureaucracy." Businessmen resented federal regulation. Conservatives worried about the impact of paternalistic government on individual self-reliance, on community responsibility, and on economic and personal freedom. The nation, in effect, renewed the old debate between Hamilton and Jefferson in the early republic.

Since the 1980s, with the presidency of Ronald Reagan, this debate has burst out with unusual intensity. According to conservatives, government intervention abridges liberty, stifles enterprise, and is inefficient, wasteful, and arbitrary. It disturbs the harmony of the self-adjusting market and creates worse troubles than it solves. "Get government off our backs," according to the popular cliché, and our problems will solve themselves. When government is necessary, let it be at the local level, close to the people.

In fact, for all the talk about the "swollen" and "bloated" bureaucracy, the federal establishment has not been growing as inexorably as many Americans seem to believe. In 1949, it consisted of 2.1 million people. Nearly 70 years later, while the country had grown by 177 million, the federal force is the same. Federal workers were a smaller percentage of the population in 2017 than they were in 1985, 1955, or 1940. The federal establishment, in short, has not kept pace with population growth. Moreover, national defense and security-related agencies account for nearly 70 percent of federal employment.

Why, then, the widespread idea about the remorseless growth of government? It is partly because in the 1960s, the national government assumed new and intrusive functions: affirmative action in civil rights, environmental protection, safety and health in the workplace, community organization, legal aid to the poor. Although this enlargement of the federal regulatory role was accompanied by marked growth in the size of government on all levels, the expansion has taken place primarily in state and local government. Whereas the federal force increased by only 27 percent in the 30 years after 1950, the state and local government forces increased by an astonishing 212 percent.

In general, Americans do not want less government. What they want is *more efficient* government. For a time in the 1970s, with the Vietnam War and Watergate, Americans lost confidence in the national government. In 1964, more than three-quarters of those polled had thought the national government could be trusted to do right most of the time. By 1980, only one-quarter was prepared to offer such trust. After reaching a three-decade high in the wake of the 9/11 terrorist attacks, public confidence in the federal government was near historic lows in 2017 at just 18 percent.

Two hundred years after the drafting of the Constitution, Americans still regard government with a mixture of reliance and mistrust—a good combination. Mistrust is the best way to keep government reliable. Informed criticism is the means of correcting governmental inefficiency, incompetence, and arbitrariness; that is, of best enabling government to play its essential role. For without government, we cannot attain the goals of the Founding Fathers. Without an understanding of government, we cannot have the informed criticism that makes government do the job right. It is the duty of every American citizen to know our government—which is what this series is all about.

Party Politics

In the earliest years of America's history as an independent nation, the country was unified behind its leadership. George Washington was the unanimous choice as the nation's first president. His **cabinet** featured many men who had figured prominently in the Continental Congress and the American Revolution, men who had stood firmly united in the effort to win independence from Great Britain.

This spirit of unity and common purpose would not last, however. In Washington's cabinet were men whose differences would soon become so great that they would form political parties to clarify their views and positions on the key issues of the day. One of these issues was precisely how power would be balanced in the new nation. Would the United States have a strong central government, or would the greater power remain with the individual state governments?

Before he was the unanimous choice as the leader of the nation, George Washington was an esteemed general and commander-in-chief of the army throughout the Revolutionary War.

George Washington's cabinet featured many men who had figured prominently in the American Revolution. The first cabinet, from 1978, is shown above: Henry Knox, Thomas Jefferson, Edmund Jennings Randolph, Alexander Hamilton, and George Washington.

Washington's secretary of the treasury, Alexander Hamilton, supported the idea of a strong central government. The political party he formed became known as the Federalist Party. Thomas Jefferson, Washington's secretary of state, believed that a strong central government would quickly become as oppressive to its citizens as the British had been to American colonists. Jefferson favored a government in which the majority of the power would be held by the individual states. Jefferson wanted the new nation to become a republic—a country in which power is held by the voting citizens and by the representatives they choose—and for this reason, his political party was known as the Republican Party.

Soon, other issues sparked greater divisions within Washington's cabinet. First was the question of whether the Bill of Rights should be added to the U.S. Constitution or not. Jefferson's Republicans supported the addition of the Bill of Rights; Hamilton's Federalists opposed it.

Economic policies were another area of disagreement. In the years after the Revolutionary War, America was struggling with debt owed to Americans who had served in the Continental Army and provided it with supplies, as well as to foreign nations that had helped with the Revolution. Hamilton thought that the national government should assume the responsibility of paying all war debts, both those of the nation and those of the individual states. Hamilton's plan to pay off these debts involved a tax on imported goods and on certain American-manufactured items, including whiskey. In addition, Hamilton argued for the creation of a national bank—one bank that would oversee the banks of the individual states. Jefferson and his Republicans strongly opposed these economic policies.

Foreign policy was yet another area that sparked debate. As war brewed in Europe, Jefferson and Hamilton disagreed on what America's position should be. In 1790, the United States government learned that Spanish naval vessels had taken command of British ships off of Vancouver Island in Canada. Jefferson argued that America's position should be one of neutrality: not supporting either side but instead continuing to do business with as many nations as possible. Hamilton disagreed; he eventually met with an agent of the British government in Canada and indicated that America might support Great Britain in the event of war. In 1792, when war broke out between France and Great Britain, the split between the two men widened. Joined by Vice President John Adams, Hamilton argued that America should support Great Britain—its major trading partner—in the conflict. Jefferson felt that America owed a debt to France for its support in the Revolutionary War.

In his efforts to create a plan to erase the national debt, Alexander Hamilton introduced national banks. In addition, he assembled a group of bankers and businessmen—friends of the government—that transformed into the Federalist Party.

These two powerful men soon persuaded other political leaders to take sides on the issues of the day. Those who, like Jefferson, believed that any powers not specifically granted in the Constitution to the national government should remain under the control of the individual states, were labeled "Republicans." Those who supported Hamilton in his belief that the national government should take whatever steps were necessary for the common good were known as "Federalists."

In 1796, the president and vice president were determined based on who received the largest and second-largest number of electoral votes. Federalist John Adams was elected president, and Republican Thomas Jefferson was elected vice president. The two men had once been good friends, but their very different views about how the government should be run would create an administration marked more by hostility than by unified purpose. It is difficult to imagine today a situation in which the two leading candidates from different political parties, both running for president, would then be expected to put aside their differences and work together cooperatively as president and vice president, but this is precisely what happened in 1796.

In 1798, the Federalist-controlled Congress passed a highly controversial set of policies known as the Alien and Sedition Acts. The Alien Act gave President Adams the power to expel any foreigners he felt might threaten national security. It also extended the period of time foreigners needed to live in the United States before they could apply for citizenship. The Sedition Act declared that anyone who published false statements about the president, his government, or Congress could be fined or put in prison.

Find out more about the Alien and Sedition Acts.

Jefferson was outraged. He viewed these acts as proof that the United States was moving in the direction of monarchy. He felt that the acts were attempts to silence political opposition (the majority of those fined and imprisoned under the Sedition Act were Republican newspaper editors) and violations of the constitutional guarantee of freedom of speech.

Although Jefferson was a member of the government in power, he was determined to focus on

NAME CHANGE

The party founded by Thomas Jefferson, the party formed of those who shared his Republican ideals, is today the oldest political party in the United States and is among the oldest political parties in the world. The party originally known as the Republican Party is known today by another name, however: the Democratic Party.

strengthening the Republican Party and attempting to win the presidency. At one point, the Federalists had tried to link Jefferson's Republicans with France's "radical democrats"—those whose actions during the French Revolution resulted in widespread violence and terror. The Federalists had sarcastically labeled Jefferson's Republicans "Democratic-Republicans." In 1798, the Republicans adopted this label—"Democratic-Republican Party"—as their official name.

The Election of 1800

The election of 1800—in which Thomas Jefferson and another Republican, Aaron Burr, challenged John Adams in his bid for reelection to the presidency—would prove to be one of the most significant in American history. Jefferson had devised his strategy long before the election. Two years earlier, he had begun a letter-writing campaign designed to spread his thoughts around the country. Jefferson sent letters to all of his influential Republican supporters and also to Republican newspapers. In the letters, he gave the reasons behind the political positions he had adopted. He explained why he believed that the powers of the individual states needed to be protected. He also argued against what he felt was an attempt to transfer all of the powers of the states to the federal government and the powers of the federal government to the presidency. Jefferson's letters called for a smaller, more cost-effective government, one that would use any leftover tax revenue to pay off national debt. He argued against a standing army in peacetime, expressing his belief that state **militias** were able to provide defense unless the country were invaded. Finally, the letters outlined Jefferson's support for freedom of the press and freedom of religion.

The election of 1800 was also noteworthy for the beginning of what eventually became known as "dirty campaigning." Jefferson, Burr, and Adams avoided directly criticizing each other, but their supporters were not so restrained. The candidates' supporters began using newspapers and pamphlets to criticize the candidates' policies, records, and reputations. Their characters were attacked through gossip and rumors. Jefferson's supporters attacked Adams and the Federalists for **deficit spending** and for their unfocused foreign policy. Federalists attacked Jefferson's character, labeling him "un-Christian."

When the election was over, John Adams failed to hold on to the presidency. He had received only 65 electoral votes, but Thomas Jefferson and Aaron Burr had tied—each received 73 electoral votes.

Thomas Jefferson (above) challenged John Adams in his bid for reelection in 1800. This was the first U.S. election in which political parties had nominated candidates.

Under the terms that then existed in the Constitution, a tie was to be decided in the House of Representatives, which was still dominated by Federalists. (The election had changed the balance of power, but the newly elected Republican representatives had not yet taken office.) After several days, 36 ballots, and much behind-the-scenes campaigning, Jefferson was finally chosen as the new president. Burr became the vice president.

This was a pivotal moment in American history. Political parties had nominated candidates. Candidates had run on issue platforms. Power had peacefully changed hands from one political party to another. Future presidential campaigns would forever be influenced by these events.

Yet, the election of 1800 also marked the end of an era. Before the next presidential election, the Twelfth Amendment to the Constitution would go into effect, changing the presidential electoral process so that electors would cast separate ballots to elect the president and the vice president. Jefferson's Democratic-Republican Party would become the dominant political party in the United States, returning Jefferson to the presidency in 1804, as well as ensuring the election of James Madison in 1808 and 1812 and James Monroe in 1816. By 1820, the Federalist Party—the party that had, in many ways, shaped the national government we know today—had faded away, and James Monroe ran unopposed in his reelection campaign.

Aaron Burr is probably best remembered today as the man who killed Alexander Hamilton in a pistol duel. In 1804, the decades-long bitter feud between the two men finally came to an end when Burr mortally wounded Hamilton.

Text-Dependent Questions

1. What is a republic?

2. Name one way the Federalists and the Republicans differed over economic policy.

3. What points did Thomas Jefferson make in his letter-writing campaign leading up to the election of 1800?

Research Project

Research the life of one leader of the early Federalist and another leader of the early Republican Party. Write a brief biography of each, including how they might have arrived at their political beliefs. Be sure to include how their views, policies, and actions were different, as well as any similarities.

Jefferson's Republicans

The victory of Thomas Jefferson and his Republicans over the Federalists in 1801 can be described as a win for his party. It was not simply Jefferson, the candidate, who won the election; the party's successes at publicizing their candidate's views, at campaigning, and at sensing what voters wanted also contributed to the victory.

Because the presidency had never before shifted from one political party to another, there was at first some uncertainty about how this kind of a transition would be handled: For example, would people appointed to positions by the Federalist president, John Adams, keep their jobs? Jefferson was particularly annoyed that Adams had rushed through many appointments just before leaving office.

At first—in his inaugural address—Jefferson indicated a willingness to cooperate with members of the opposition party. "We are

Thomas Jefferson's official presidential portrait was painted by Rembrandt Peale in 1800.

all Republicans—we are all Federalists," he said. Soon, though, under a certain amount of pressure from members of his party, Jefferson's position began to shift. Initially uncertain about whether to remove all or none of the Federalists in office, he gradually decided to ensure that his fellow Republicans held about two-thirds of all political jobs. Federalists were removed from office and replaced with Republicans to achieve this balance. Those whom Adams had appointed at the last minute were the first to go.

Jefferson's party was noteworthy for its organization. This depended, in large part, on the Republican members of Congress, who supplied the party's leadership in Congress and also, through connections in their home states, helped maintain a consistent message for local and state organizations.

Washington, D.C., was a new capital—and a new city—when Jefferson became president, and few congressmen had homes there. Instead, they lived and ate together in boardinghouses. Over breakfasts and dinners, they had heated discussions and hammered out the key issues of the day. The representatives usually socialized with members of their own party—taverns and boardinghouses tended to attract either Republican or Federalist customers, but seldom both.

Vice President

For the election of 1804, it was clear that Thomas Jefferson would once more be his party's nominee for president. Leaders of the Republican Party decided to focus on their nominee for vice president.

The Twelfth Amendment had not yet been **ratified** (although it ultimately would be ratified before the election), so there was not yet a system in place for nominating both the president and vice president on a single ballot. Instead, the old system still was in use. Whoever received more electoral votes would become president; the runner-up would be vice president. Republicans wanted to select a potential vice president who was popular and appealing enough to surpass all other candidates but not so strong that he would get more votes than Jefferson.

Aaron Burr, Jefferson's vice president in his first term, was not considered for the ticket this time. Burr and Jefferson had initially tied in the election of 1800, and Jefferson had always questioned Burr's loyalty and largely ignored him during the

JEFFERSON'S FIRST INAUGURAL ADDRESS

On March 4, 1801, Thomas Jefferson became the first president to be inaugurated in the new capital of Washington, D.C. In his inaugural address, he spoke of the bitter campaign that had preceded the election:

. . . We have called by different names brethren of the same principle. We are all Republicans, we are all Federalists. . . . Let us then, with courage and confidence pursue our own Federal and Republican principles, our attachment to union and representative government. Kindly separated by nature and a wide ocean from the exterminating havoc of one quarter of the globe; too high-minded to endure the degradations of the others; possessing a chosen country, with room enough for our descendants to the thousandth and thousandth generation; entertaining a due sense of our equal right to the use of our own faculties, to the acquisitions of our own industry, to honor and confidence from our fellow-citizens, resulting not from birth, but from our actions and their sense of them; enlightened by a benign religion, professed, indeed, and practiced in various forms, yet all of them inculcating honesty, truth, temperance, gratitude, and the love of man; acknowledging and adoring an overruling Providence, which by all its dispensations proves that it delights in the happiness of man here and his greater happiness hereafter—with all these blessings, what more is necessary to make us a happy and a prosperous people? Still one thing more, fellow-citizens—a wise and frugal Government, which shall restrain men from injuring one another, shall leave them otherwise free to regulate their own pursuits of industry and improvement, and shall not take from the mouth of labor the bread it has earned. This is the sum of good government. . . .

Source: "Thomas Jefferson First Inaugural Address." The Avalon Project at Yale Law School. Available online. URL: http://avalon.law.yale.edu/19th_century/jefinau1.asp. Updated on March 4, 2007.

Thomas Jefferson was the first president to be inaugurated in Washington, D.C. This painting depicts what the Capitol of Washington looked like in 1800 before it was burned to the ground by the British.

first term. While serving as vice president, Burr ran for election as governor of New York but was defeated. Later, he was involved in a duel with Alexander Hamilton that resulted in Hamilton's death.

In February 1804, a group of Republicans gathered and nominated a committee of men whose goal was to "promote the success of the Republican nominations." Thirteen men were chosen for the committee: Seven were senators, and six were members of the House of Representatives, and they were from 13 different states. Their mission was not only to ensure Thomas Jefferson's reelection but also to guarantee that his vice president was a supportive Republican.

This was a significant development in party politics, as this group of 13 men represented the first formal national party organization established to elect a president and vice president. The party's ultimate choice for the vice-presidential candidate was the governor of New York, George Clinton. In addition to his experience and political prominence, Clinton added geographical balance to a ticket whose presidential candidate came from Virginia.

The party was particularly eager to focus its attention on the New England states. Before 1800, New England had been strongly Federalist. During Jefferson's presidency, his party concentrated its efforts on ensuring that the Republican Party was not merely a Southern political party, but a national party.

Party organizations were set up in each state. By October 1801, instructions had been given out to party organizers in each town. These party committees were told to make up a list of all those eligible to vote in their towns, especially those likely to consider themselves Republican. The committees were told to hold a private meeting of these Republicans and to discuss with them the importance of ensuring that Republican principles were maintained in local government. The committees were also told to try to make sure that Republican newspapers were circulated in their towns. These early organizations formed the basis of party structure at the local level.

In 1804, when Jefferson sought reelection, his party reminded voters of the failures of Federalist President John Adams and provided a list of Jefferson's accomplishments during his four years in office. These included reduction of taxes, elimination of several thousand unnecessary government jobs, reduction of the national debt, maintenance of peace, and the purchase of the Louisiana territory. It is interesting to note that, apart from the Louisiana Purchase, many similar claims feature in modern presidential campaigns.

Adams and the Federalists were also linked—unfavorably—to Great Britain. The Revolutionary War was still recent history, and voters were reminded that Great Britain had been America's greatest enemy not long ago. Federalists responded by linking their party to George Washington. They organized a large public celebration of George Washington's birthday and described a vote for the Federalist candidates as a vote for the "Washington ticket."

In the end, Jefferson was overwhelmingly successful in his bid for reelection. He won every state except Delaware and Connecticut.

Jefferson's Successor

There was pressure on Jefferson to run for a third term as president when the election of 1808 drew closer. He was the clear leader of his party: Its goals had been shaped by his vision for the country.

Jefferson's second term had not been as smooth or peaceful as his first term, however, and there was growing conflict with Great Britain. Jefferson believed that the country was now set on a course that would ensure its long-term success. He wanted to spend his remaining years at his home in Virginia.

Three men vied for the Republican nomination once it became clear that Jefferson would not run for a third term: Secretary of State James Madison, Vice President George Clinton, and James Monroe. Some people used this competition to try to persuade Jefferson to change his mind. They wanted him to seek a third term in order to prevent a split in the party he had founded. Jefferson held firm, though, and made it clear that Madison was his choice as a successor. Ultimately, George Clinton was nominated by the party as Madison's running mate.

Madison faced the same Federalist candidate who had challenged Thomas Jefferson in 1804: Charles Pinckney of South Carolina. Jefferson's party again triumphed. Madison won 122 electoral votes to Pinckney's 44. The party had held the presidency for eight years and ensured its transition to a new president. It was a clear demonstration that the values and positions of the party mattered as much to the voters as did the personal appeal of Thomas Jefferson. It was also a demonstration of the party's success at transmitting its message to the voters.

Madison in Office

Much of the Republican Party's early success had been based on the leadership offered by members of Congress; however, the split that had resulted in three different men vying for the presidency reflected a split in the Republican congressional leadership, as well. Each candidate had his own backers in Congress, and the supporters of Monroe and Clinton were less willing to work with Madison because he was not "their" candidate.

For this reason, Madison began his presidency facing greater challenges than those Jefferson had encountered during his first months in office. Madison was aware of the importance of ensuring support from Congress, and as a result he tried

In 1808, James Madison, the Republican candidate for president, won 122 electoral votes and the presidency. He was the nation's fourth president and was reelected to a second term.

to please various factions by appointing their nominees to governmental positions, regardless of their skills or abilities.

Learn about the life of James Madison.

Jefferson had clearly been the party's leader during his presidency. Under Madison, leadership of the party seemed more firmly held by Congress members. Conflict with Great Britain soon made it clear that war was likely; the Federalists pounced on this, proclaiming themselves to be the "party of peace," whereas Madison's Republicans were described as the "war party."

American forces were not adequately prepared for the War of 1812. In the midterm elections, many of the older Republicans in Congress had been replaced by new, younger candidates. These younger congressmen had not experienced the Revolutionary War firsthand, so the America they knew was very different from that of men like Jefferson and Madison. Many of them were Southerners and Westerners, and they elected Henry Clay of Kentucky as speaker of the house. Their focus was on expanding American territory. They had not lived through a war with Great Britain, and as a result, their expectations for the war were optimistic, even unrealistic. Thus, Congress did not act quickly when it came to building up the navy or raising taxes to provide funds for the military campaign.

The likelihood that Madison would lead the country into war created a split within the party and the country as the presidential election of 1812 drew close. A vote for Madison equaled, in the minds of some voters, a vote for war with England. A group of Republicans from New York broke away from the party and nominated DeWitt Clinton as their candidate for president. Clinton won all of the New England states, with one exception—Vermont—and all of the Middle Atlantic states except Pennsylvania. Madison won by only 39 electoral votes, scarcely an endorsement for his policies or his presidency.

The Republicans benefited from a weak Federalist Party; otherwise Madison might not have been reelected. Still, the party faced internal **schisms**: a split between Republicans of different ages and from different regions of the country and a split between those who favored war and those who favored peace. The

The Battle of New Orleans, depicted in the illustration above, contributed to Andrew Jackson's reputation as a war hero. He led troops made up of volunteers, free blacks, slaves, and French pirates to defeat the British.

definitions that had once separated the nation into Republicans and Federalists were no longer clear, replaced by other definitions of how the future of the country should be shaped.

America at War

In 1814, the British launched attacks in New York and in New Orleans. They attacked cities along the Atlantic coast, and by August, British ships were sailing up the Potomac River to Washington, D.C., where they burned the White

House and the Capitol. President Madison was forced to flee to Virginia. It was a humiliation for the president but one that served to rally the nation behind the war effort.

One of the most significant battles in the war was fought in New Orleans, where General Andrew Jackson defeated the British with a force made up of volunteers, slaves, free blacks, and about 1,000 French pirates. The battle would prove to be one of the most decisive of the war, and Jackson's triumphs would make him a war hero and later an important political figure.

There was one last internal challenge that Madison needed to settle while the war was still being fought. Several New England states (including Vermont, Massachusetts, Rhode Island, and Connecticut) were dissatisfied with Madison's leadership. They decided to protest the war, debated **secession** (separating from the rest of the United States), and chose to negotiate a separate peace with England. They sent representatives to Washington, D.C., to present their demands. When the representatives arrived, they learned of Jackson's defeat of the British at New Orleans and that a peace treaty had been signed in Belgium. Madison could have publicly humiliated the states for their disloyalty, but instead he allowed the representatives to return home quietly. Nevertheless, the action was perceived to be a Federalist effort and contributed to a further decline of the Federalist Party.

James Monroe

As Madison's second term in office came to an end, the Republican nominating committee chose James Monroe as Madison's successor. Daniel Tompkins, the former governor of New York, was chosen as his running mate. Some Republicans grumbled about a "Virginia dynasty"—like Madison and Jefferson, Monroe was a Virginia native—but the only serious challenger Monroe faced for the Republican nomination was another Southerner, William Crawford, who had also been born in Virginia. The Republicans had hit on a winning formula: a presidential candidate from Virginia whose running mate was a former governor of New York. Monroe easily won election over his Federalist challenger, Rufus King of New York, who made no effort to campaign and won only three states (Massachusetts, Connecticut, and Delaware) to Monroe's 16.

The presidential portrait of James Monroe.

The ease with which Monroe had won election and the general disarray of the Federalists seemed to suggest that America would evolve into a single-party nation—or perhaps a nation with no political parties at all. Andrew Jackson, serving as commander of the federal army in the South, suggested to Monroe that he bring an end to the party system by ignoring party affiliation when choosing his cabinet. Monroe was not yet willing to do so; however, he did choose John Quincy Adams, son of the last Federalist president, to serve as his secretary of state.

Monroe began his presidency with a tour of the states; he was the first president to do so since George Washington. His tour prompted such a favorable response from the people, who relished the opportunity to see their president, that the early years of his presidency were soon being described as the "Era of Good Feelings." The country continued to expand to the south and west, and four new states—Alabama, Illinois, Indiana, and Mississippi—joined the Union.

Most Americans were still farmers, although industry was growing, particularly in the Northeast. Monroe traveled to the West several times, and during his presidency the western boundary of the United States was set at the Pacific Ocean. In addition, the territory of Florida was granted to the United States in a treaty with Spain.

Slavery was gradually becoming the focus of more intense political debates. It was an issue that would deeply affect Monroe's party—the party that would eventually become the Democratic Party. Under Monroe's presidency, the issue that would transform the Union first began to divide North and South.

Text-Dependent Questions

1. Who was the Republican Party's ultimate choice for the vice-presidential candidate in 1804?

2. Name two of the accomplishments of his first term that Jefferson touted while running for reelection in 1804.

3. Why were the years following James Monroe's election described as the "Era of Good Feelings"?

Research Project

Research the history of the War of 1812, including its causes, major battles and military leaders, and eventual outcome. Create an annotated timeline of the war's events that includes relevant information. Bonus: Draw a map to illustrate the movements of troops during one of the battles highlighted in your timeline.

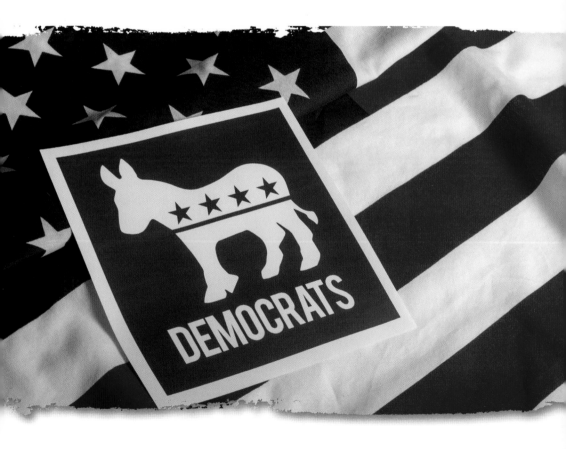

A Party Divided

Words to Understand

Aristocracy: The highest class of a society; a form of government in which this class is allowed to rule.

Caucus: A gathering of members of a specific political party or organization to form policy positions, choose leaders, and make other decisions relevant to the organization.

Colonize: When people from one country settle in and take control over another country, territory, or land.

In 1819, the Missouri Territory petitioned to join the Union as a state. At the time, the country was evenly split into states that permitted slavery and those that did not, with 11 on each side. The Constitution had stated that the issue of whether or not to allow slavery was up to each individual state. Republican congressman James Talmadge of New York, however, suggested that Missouri's petition to join the Union contain an amendment stating that no additional slaves could be brought into the state and that those who were already there would eventually be set free.

This proposal launched a fierce debate in Congress. Southern congressmen argued that each state had the right to decide whether or not to permit slavery. The debate was finally resolved with a compromise in March 1820. Missouri could join the United States as a slave state, but Maine would also join as a free state. Additional laws were passed to ban

In 1819, slavery was beginning to seriously divide the nation. At that time, slave owners could do as they pleased with their slaves. This painting depicts a slave owner tracking down a slave who had run away.

The committee of Conference of the Senate and of the House of Representatives, on the subject of the disagreeing votes of the Two Houses, upon the Bill entitled an "Act for the admission of the State of Maine into the Union".

Report the following Resolution.

Resolved.

1st That they recommend to the Senate to recede from their amendments to the said Bill

2d That they recommend to the two Houses to agree to strike out of the fourth section of the Bill from the House of Representatives now pending in the Senate, entitled an "Act to authorize the people of the Missouri Territory to form a Constitution and State Government and for the admission of such State into the Union upon an equal footing with the original States". The following proviso in the following words — and shall ordain and establish, that there shall be neither Slavery nor involuntary Servitude otherwise than in the punishment of crimes whereof the party shall have been duly convicted: provided always, That any person escaping into the same, from whom labour or service is lawfully claimed in any other State such fugitive may be lawfully reclaimed, and conveyed to the person claiming his or her labour or service, as aforesaid: Provided nevertheless, That the said Provision shall not be construed to alter the condition or civil rights of any person now held to service or labor in the said Territory."

And that the following provision be added to the Bill –

And be it further enacted, That in all that Territory ceded by France to the United States under the name of Louisiana, which lies north of thirty six degrees and thirty minutes north latitude, not included within the limits of the State contemplated by this act, Slavery and involuntary servitude otherwise than in the punishment of crimes whereof the party shall have been duly convicted, shall be and is hereby

When the Missouri Territory petitioned to join the United States, the nation was evenly split between states that permitted slavery and those that did not. The Missouri Compromise of 1820 allowed Missouri in as a slave state while Maine joined the Union as a free state.

slavery in all remaining territory acquired in the Louisiana Purchase, north of a specific line of latitude. Many political figures—including John Quincy Adams and Thomas Jefferson—saw the Missouri Compromise as a dangerous sign of division within the United States, where lines that separated slave states from free states were drawn.

Today, the Missouri Compromise is viewed as a political mistake. In 1820, however, as Monroe sought reelection, his administration's policies were viewed favorably—so favorably, in fact, that the Republican members of Congress felt that it was not necessary to discuss nominations: Monroe was the clear choice. The Federalists were unable to mount any kind of real challenge. America had become essentially a one-party country, and that one party was the Democratic-Republican Party. Monroe received all but one of the Electoral College votes; that single vote went to John Quincy Adams. It is interesting to note that President John Adams, John Quincy's father and a member of the Electoral College, was not responsible for casting that single vote. He voted for Monroe.

In Monroe's second term, he developed the foreign policy position that would become a defining achievement in America's role in global affairs. Known as the Monroe Doctrine, the policy was created in response to Monroe's effort to support the independence recently declared by former Spanish and Portuguese colonies in Latin America. Monroe was determined not only to support the independence of these nations but also to firmly state to the European powers that the United States would oppose any further attempt to **colonize** lands in the Western Hemisphere.

This significant achievement took place during Monroe's second term, but the end of his presidency was also beset by confusion within his party. Power to nominate presidential candidates had been held firmly by congressional Republicans, but their power was slipping away as state legislatures assumed a greater role in party politics. In addition, with more and more eligible voters—that is, white males—the focus of the party shifted toward appealing to those voters in a more direct way.

A Divisive Election

Campaigning for the election of 1824 began two years earlier, as various candidates began to position themselves to receive their parties' nominations. At one point, there were as many as 16 potential candidates for the Republican Party's nomination.

Gradually, they were whittled down to six and then to four: Secretary of State John Quincy Adams, the former Federalist from Massachusetts; William Crawford, the secretary of the treasury; Henry Clay, the Speaker of the House of Representatives; and Andrew Jackson, the military hero who had been elected as a senator from Tennessee.

The party that had been so disciplined in bringing Thomas Jefferson, James Madison, and James Monroe to office had lost its focus. Chaos reigned as competing interests lobbied for their candidates.

Without party organization supporting a particular candidate, the election proved to be a mess. Voter turnout was very low, little more than 25 percent. Andrew Jackson led in both the electoral and popular votes, but by such a small number that he failed to achieve the

THE ELECTORAL COLLEGE

Presidents are elected based not on the number of popular votes they receive, but on the number of electoral votes. Each state has a certain number of electors (representatives to the Electoral College) who cast votes for that state. The number is based on the number of senators from the state (always two) and the number of U.S. representatives (which varies from state to state based on population).

In the presidential election, the party whose candidate has won the most popular votes in a state wins all the electors of that state. The exceptions to this are Maine and Nebraska—two electors are chosen by statewide popular vote and the remainder are chosen by the popular vote within each congressional district.

Because certain states have more congressional representatives, these states have more electors. Presidential campaigns often focus on states with the most electoral votes—California is the largest, with 55. Other key states include Texas (34), New York (31), Florida (27), Pennsylvania and Illinois (21 each), and Ohio (20). The candidate for president with the most electoral votes (it must be at least one more than half of the total) is declared president.

necessary majority of electoral votes. This meant that the election had to be decided in the House of Representatives. According to the Constitution, only the leading three candidates were to be considered. Clay had received the fewest electoral votes, so he was eliminated. Crawford was suffering from a serious illness, misdiagnosed as a stroke, so he, too, was not considered in the House. The contest came down to John Quincy Adams and Andrew Jackson.

Clay was soon the focus of intense lobbying efforts by backers of Adams and Jackson, who wanted his support for their candidates. Clay did not like Jackson, however, and did not think that he had the qualifications to serve as president. Clay

President Adams' Secretary of State, Henry Clay.

met several times with Adams and ultimately gave his support (and his electoral votes) to Adams, who was then declared to be president. Jackson and his supporters were outraged and declared that some sort of secret deal had been made to steal the election from the man who had received the most votes. Their suspicions seemed to be proved correct when, shortly after Adams was elected, he appointed Clay to serve as his secretary of state.

This difficult beginning marked much of John Quincy Adams's presidency. His credibility damaged by the suggestion that the election had not been fairly

The sixth president of the United States, John Quincy Adams (above), was the son of the second president, John Adams. Quincy Adams had a difficult presidency; in particular, he found it hard to work with Congress.

won, Adams found it difficult to work with Congress. His party—his adopted party, since he had once been a Federalist—had been hurt by the election and split into various groups. Many congressmen were outspoken in their criticism of Adams: Martin Van Buren, a senator from New York, and John Randolph, a senator from Virginia, were among the worst. In fact, Randolph was so outspoken in his criticism of the Adams administration, and Secretary of State Clay in particular, that Clay eventually challenged Randolph to a duel. The senator and secretary of state fired at each other, but Randolph's cloak received the only damage from this exchange of gunfire.

Adams's presidency was marked by such intense disagreement among members of his own party that his single term in office can be viewed today as the end of an era. The Republican Party that had produced four presidents would be forever changed in the years that followed: it would be divided in two. Supporters of Clay and older members of the party renamed themselves the National Republicans. Andrew Jackson led the other group that split from the party. That group was known as the Democratic Party, the name by which the party is known today.

The Party of the People

The party founded by Thomas Jefferson had first come into power claiming itself as the "party of the people." The presidents who had been elected by this party, however, owed perhaps less to the people than to a select group of men: the congressional Republican **caucus** (nominating committee). Jefferson, Monroe, and Madison represented a distinct type—Virginians and well-educated, wealthy men who had played a role in America since its founding. With Madison, Monroe, and even Adams, a standard had been set. A politician would spend a certain amount of time serving in a president's cabinet and then essentially be selected by that president as his successor.

With the election of Andrew Jackson in 1828, the party—and the presidency—entered a new phase. For one thing, voters played a greater role than ever before in ensuring the election of Jackson. Gradually, since 1810, the voting policies in states had been changing. In the oldest states, voting had been restricted to those who owned property of some sort or paid taxes. As new states joined the Union, this began to change, and gradually one state after another began to shift its voting policies so that the right to vote was given to all white males over the age of 21.

This was an incredibly important shift. Once, presidents had been chosen based on connections and political influence, but suddenly a candidate could appeal directly to the voters, who could use their influence to select the candidate who most appealed to them. In 1828, Andrew Jackson was that candidate. The brash war hero was tremendously popular, and many viewed the election of 1824 as having been "stolen" from him.

Gradually, the split in the Republican Party had begun to emerge. Martin Van Buren perhaps first contributed to the split, although he did so to advance his candidate (Jackson). In 1827, he gathered a committee of men in Nashville whose aim was to communicate with other "Jackson committees" in other parts of the country.

At the time, candidates for the presidency did not actively campaign for office—it was not regarded as dignified. The campaigning was left to their supporters, and Van Buren was more than willing to campaign actively on Jackson's behalf. Jackson certainly presented a more colorful image than Adams. In addition to his reputation as a military hero, Jackson proudly described himself as a rough "backwoodsman." Jackson's nickname, "Old Hickory," became the basis for a whole campaign. Hickory Clubs were organized, and hickory trees were planted at political rallies. Political souvenirs such as plates, pitchers, and ladies' hair combs were all stamped with pictures of Jackson.

The contest between Adams and Jackson was described by Jackson supporters as a contest between democracy and **aristocracy**—Jackson, of course, represented the side of democracy. Newspapers that supported one side or the other published gossip and rumors about both men.

Jackson's campaign as a "common man" proved victorious, with especially strong support in the South and West. Adams took New England, but Jackson won nearly every other state except Delaware, Maryland, and New Jersey.

President Jackson

Jackson entered the presidency with little political experience; he had been elected in large part because of his military career, rather than his career as a senator. It is important to note that although he was the first American president raised in humble circumstances, he was not poor when elected to office. He cultivated his image as a backwoodsman and frontiersman, but Jackson had established a successful career and achieved great wealth in his lifetime—he had built a fortune speculating in land. His home was a mansion near Nashville, and he owned slaves.

Jackson created for his party what came to be known as "Jacksonian Democracy," a philosophy that had much in common with Jefferson's idealized vision of an America of hardworking farmers and planters. Jackson's presidential policies would reflect this preference for agriculture as the most important occupation and his disregard for the wealthy. Under Jackson, federal jobs were deliberately handed out to those who shared his political views.

When Jackson sought reelection in 1832, the split between members of his party was complete. The more traditional wing of the party labeled itself the National Republicans. Jackson and his supporters wanted to clearly distinguish themselves from this group. They took the name "Democratic Party" to demonstrate their connection to the concept of democracy.

The first national conventions were held for this election. The National Republicans held their convention in December 1831. Their nominee for the presidency was Henry Clay. Five months later, 334 Democrats met in Baltimore. They represented every state except Missouri, and their unanimous choice was Jackson, with Martin Van Buren as his running mate.

This convention was an important milestone for the Democratic Party. Procedures were set up for future conventions and future nominations, ensuring that this was not Jackson's party but one that would endure beyond a single election or a single candidate. Majority rule dictated which candidate would be chosen. Two-thirds of the delegates needed to approve not only the presidential but also the vice-presidential nominee.

Jackson easily won reelection, and the Democratic Party was established not as a branch of the Republican Party but as a political party in its own right. Thanks to Jackson, it was identified as the party of the common man; the wealthy and the elite were labeled its opponents. The Democratic Party still retains some of this image today.

In his second term, Jackson challenged the national bank system, shifting federal money from the national bank to a series of state banks. The banking issue prompted a group of businessmen and opponents of Jackson's to band together in an effort to oppose the man they labeled "King Andrew I." They called themselves "Whigs," after the British political party formed to oppose the king of England in the 1700s. Soon, they would develop into a political force, particularly in New England.

Jackson's presidency was marked by prosperity, but his economic policies would prove problematic for his successor. Jackson disliked paper money and insisted that, when public lands were sold, payment could be made only with gold or silver.

It was also under Jackson that many Native Americans were forcibly moved from their native lands in Georgia to the so-called "Indian Territory" in the West.

uncommitted to any other course than the strict line of constitutional duty; and that the securities for this independence may be rendered as strong as the nature of power and the weakness of its possessor will admit, — I cannot too earnestly invite your attention to the propriety of promoting such an amendment of the constitution as will render him ineligible after one term of service.

It gives me pleasure to announce to Congress that the benevolent policy of the Government, steadily pursued for nearly thirty years in relation to the removal

In 1830, President Jackson signed the Indian Removal Act, which ultimately forced American Indians to the South. The land became known as "Indian Territory" and changed the lives of Indians for years to come. The Cherokee refused these orders. Eventually, they were defeated and forcibly marched west on what became known as the Trail of Tears.

THE DEMOCRATIC PARTY

The aim was to open up Southern land for cotton planting. The Supreme Court tried to protect the Native Americans, but Jackson defied the court and ordered federal troops to escort the tribes to the West.

Andrew Jackson, Native Americans, and the Trail of Tears.

Martin Van Buren

In 1836, the Democrats again gathered in Baltimore. Vice President Martin Van Buren, the man who had masterminded Jackson's campaign, was the party's choice for president. Richard Mentor Johnson of Kentucky was Jackson's choice for vice president, and the party followed his wishes.

Van Buren was the son of a tavern keeper from the small village of Kinderhook, New York. He had become a leader in New York state politics in what was then the Republican Party, and although eventually elected senator, he remained in close touch with his state organization. Van Buren understood the importance of an organized, disciplined state party, and he had helped develop this organization as the Democratic Party was formed.

Van Buren had put his full effort into ensuring Jackson's election, and Jackson returned the favor by campaigning for Van Buren. Van Buren was an experienced politician—far more experienced than Jackson had been—and he believed deeply in the Democratic Party. He felt that the Democratic Party's principles—low taxes, no national debt, states' rights, and strict interpretation of the Constitution—should be clearly expressed to voters.

Van Buren's hope was that the party's convention would focus on these ideas. Instead, the convention's message to voters—the type of message that would eventually be known as the party's platform—focused on party heroes like Jefferson, Madison, Monroe, and Jackson. Van Buren, the actual nominee, was mentioned only once.

Despite Jackson's support for his candidacy and the backing of the organized Democratic Party structure, Van Buren barely won the popular vote, earning 50.9 percent. He did, however, receive a majority of the electoral votes and assumed the presidency in 1837.

The Democratic Party had been shaped by Van Buren but was transformed by events in the nation and by Jackson's appeal to voters. Whereas congressional caucuses had once played a key role in choosing the candidate, the national convention had assumed that function, and not only national but also local and state politicians now played an important role in party politics.

Under Jackson, the Democratic Party had become, in a sense, a party that had achieved success because of the president's willingness to divide Americans. Jackson drew a distinction between the wealthy and the poor, and the laborers and the business owners, and even divided Southerners and Westerners from those in the East.

Jackson's legacy was a challenging one for Van Buren who, though a seasoned politician, had none of Jackson's charisma. Van Buren was further burdened by the legacy of Jackson's economic policies. Only weeks after Van Buren took office, New York banks began to cut back on loans in an effort to bring a halt to widespread speculation. Soon, banks across the country followed suit, and a panic resulted in the worst depression the nation had known. Banks and businesses closed down, and unemployment rose to record levels. Van Buren insisted on following Jackson's policies of accepting only hard currency (gold and silver) rather than paper money, refusing to charter a national bank or taking steps that could stem the crisis.

The Whig Party was quick to seize on the opportunity offered by the financial crisis. They labeled the president "Martin Van Ruin" and selected William Henry Harrison as their candidate in the 1840 presidential campaign. The Whigs skillfully presented Harrison as a candidate similar to Jackson—a military hero who had defeated the British at the Battle of the Thames. Harrison was given the nickname "Old Tippecanoe" and was presented as another self-made candidate of humble beginnings, with images of a log cabin often appearing on posters that advertised his candidacy. There was little truth in this political image making. Harrison was the son of an aristocratic Virginia family and had lived on an impressive estate in the Ohio countryside. In fact, Van Buren's childhood had been far humbler than Harrison's. Nonetheless, Van Buren was depicted by the Whigs as a polished, elegantly dressed politician and contrasted with their candidate who, they claimed, liked nothing more than a swig of hard cider from a jug. Campaign speakers suggested to voters that the choice was "between the log cabin and the palace, between hard cider and champagne." Harrison's running mate was John Tyler of Virginia, who had been a Democrat but left the party after disagreeing with many of Jackson's policies.

The Democratic convention was held in Baltimore in May 1840. It was at this convention that the party's name was officially changed from the Democratic-Republican Party to the Democratic Party. The party nominated Van Buren but did not name a vice-presidential candidate.

The Whigs proved their mastery of the campaign, using the symbols of the log cabin and cider jugs to promote their candidate and transform the election into entertainment. Nearly 80 percent of all those eligible to vote did so in the election. Van Buren lost. The era of Jacksonian Democracy had come to an end.

Text-Dependent Questions

1. What were the stipulations of the Missouri Compromise?

2. Name one reason why voters played a greater role in the election of Andrew Jackson in 1828 than they did in previous elections.

3. Which native American tribe was subjected to the Trail of Tears?

Research Project

Research the birthplace or homestead of one of the presidents mentioned in this chapter, including John Quincy Adams's birthplace at Adams National Historic Park, Andrew Jackson's Hermitage, or Martin Van Buren's Lindenwald. Write a brief report about the place, including its location, a description of its architecture and furnishings, the history of its ownership, and other significant information.

Slavery and the Democratic Party

By the middle of the nineteenth century, slavery was emerging as an issue of increasing political focus. The question about whether or not slavery should be permitted was nothing new to political debate, but by the mid-1800s, more and more focus was placed on how to respond to slavery.

For the election of 1840, in which Martin Van Buren was defeated in his bid for reelection, a group of **abolitionists** (activists who attempted to have slavery outlawed) formed their own political party—the Liberty Party—and nominated their own candidate for president. Although their bid for the presidency was unsuccessful, it was a sign that slavery was becoming an issue that presidential candidates would need to address. That issue would prove particularly disastrous for the Democratic Party.

From 1841 to 1845, the Whigs occupied the White House. William Henry Harrison served as president for only a month before dying of pneumonia. He was the first president to die in office. John Tyler, the

Martin van Buren, the eighth president of the United States, was one of the founders of the Democratic Party.

vice president, became president. The former Democrat struggled to work with the Whig Congress members; their disgust with his policies became so strong that the Whigs ultimately decided to expel Tyler from their party. An **impeachment** resolution was introduced in the House of Representatives, but it failed to pass.

When the Democratic convention was again held in Baltimore, President Tyler sent representatives to suggest that he should be nominated by the Democrats. Martin Van Buren also sought the nomination, but his outspoken position on whether or not Texas should be annexed (forcibly added) by the United States (he was opposed, fearing that it would spark a war with Mexico) caused him to lose the support of most delegates.

It took several ballots before a front-runner emerged, a man who had come to the convention hoping to be nominated as vice president. James K. Polk had served

This cartoon shows Andrew Jackson leading the Democratic Party donkey, James K. Polk, and George Dallas to political disaster.

as Speaker of the House of Representatives and governor of Tennessee, yet he was essentially a little-known candidate—so much so, in fact, that the Whig campaign repeatedly posed the question, "Who is James K. Polk?"

Polk, though, sensing that most Americans wanted to see their country expand, spoke out in favor of annexing Texas and Oregon, and he had the support of the aging Andrew Jackson. Expansion became his issue, and this emphasis was popular in the South and the West. Slavery existed in the background of this issue: Texas's entry into the United States would tip the balance in favor of slaveholding states. Polk's tough stance against Mexico (which claimed Texas) and Great Britain (which claimed portions of Oregon) was also popular. He won the election and, shortly after his victory, Congress voted to annex Texas.

Polk kept to his promise of expanding the country. He signed a treaty with the British that brought Oregon in as American territory. Disputes over territory were followed by war with Mexico, but American forces were successful. In the end, Polk added not only Texas but also New Mexico and California to American territory. With this new territory, however, came the question that had haunted each American effort to expand: Would slavery be allowed in these new territories?

James Polk and the Mexican-American War.

Lines of Division

Polk himself was a slave owner. His belief was that since cotton could not grow in the soil of the American west, slavery would probably never develop there. He suggested that California be introduced into the Union as a free state to balance the slave state of Texas.

The question of slavery was moving beyond the idea of balance, however, to a broader moral question: Should the United States be a nation that allowed human beings to live in bondage? Northern Democrats were increasingly outspoken in their efforts to ensure that slavery was banned in any new territory acquired by the United States. This triggered a split with Southern Democrats, also known as "Dixie Democrats," who felt that the party was losing touch with Southern interests.

Polk had stated that, when elected, he would serve only one term. The split in the party made the choice of the party's next candidate for the presidency particularly critical.

At the 1848 convention, an antislavery group wanted to nominate Martin Van Buren. A proslavery group wanted to nominate John C. Calhoun, who had formed a Southern Rights Movement to pressure the Democratic Party and had stated that his delegates would never support a candidate who took a position against slavery. Finally, a third group, which supported Lewis Cass, favored allowing the territories to decide for themselves whether or not to permit slavery. Cass was chosen almost as a compromise candidate, in an effort to avoid alienating supporters on either end of the slavery issue. The effort would fail.

Despite the bitterness and chaos, the 1848 Democratic convention is noteworthy because at this convention, the decision was made to establish a formal Democratic National Committee, with one member for each state. It was decided that the committee would meet during congressional and presidential election years to plan and coordinate strategy.

The choice of Cass, intended as a compromise, ultimately pleased few Democrats. Van Buren and his supporters criticized their party as a "Slavocracy" and left, forming their own party in Buffalo, New York, which they called the Free Soil Party. Their platform consisted of opposition to slavery in any form in the new territories. The Free Soilers were joined by many former Whigs when that party nominated General Zachary Taylor, a hero of the Mexican War who was himself a slave owner in Louisiana.

Taylor was an unusual choice for the Whigs. He was not a Whig—in fact, he claimed that he belonged to no political party. He also stated that he had never voted in a presidential election.

Nevertheless, the Free Soilers managed to pull enough votes away from the Democratic candidate, Cass, to ultimately result in the election of Taylor in the first presidential election in which all states voted on the same day. Pro- and antislavery supporters within the Democratic Party saw the election results as evidence that their position was the correct one. The party could not afford to compromise but would need to resolve its position on slavery once and for all.

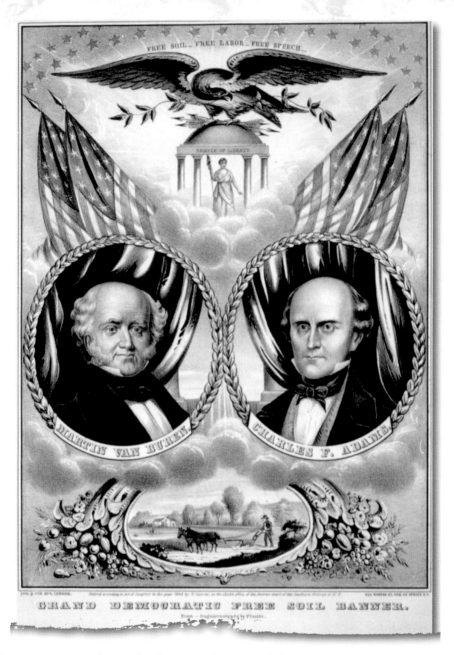

Above is a campaign banner for the Free Soil Party candidates in 1848, Martin Van Buren and Charles Adams. Van Buren and his supporters left the Democratic Party after it nominated a compromise candidate for that year's election.

THE 1850 COMPROMISE

In an effort to address the question of whether or not slavery should be permitted in newly acquired U.S. territories, President Millard Fillmore championed what became known as the 1850 Compromise. The following points were presented to the Senate as five separate bills:

1. Admit California as a free state.
2. Settle the Texas boundary by allowing New Mexico to keep most of its land and compensating Texas for the areas it had claimed.
3. Grant territorial status to New Mexico.
4. Place federal officers at the disposal of slaveholders seeking fugitive slaves.
5. Outlaw the slave trade in the District of Columbia.

Each of the bills passed, and on September 20, 1850, President Fillmore signed them into law. Although intended as a way to preserve the Union, they would only temporarily keep the peace between the North and the South.

Compromise

Taylor's solution to the slaveholding crisis was to have the new territories quickly become states. They would then vote on whether or not to permit slavery. When Southern leaders threatened that their states would leave the Union, Taylor boldly faced them down, promising to lead the army against them and to hang anyone found guilty of rebelling against the Union. Taylor collapsed after participating in a ceremony on a particularly hot July 4, however, and died a few days later. His successor, Millard Fillmore, was also a supporter of this compromise effort, but Fillmore had signed the controversial Fugitive Slave Act, which allowed slave owners to hunt down slaves who had fled to free states, capture them, and take them back into slavery.

Gathering for its convention in Baltimore in 1852, the Democratic Party vowed to resist any efforts to readdress the question of slavery in or out of Congress. Their nominee was Franklin Pierce, a former senator from New Hampshire, who had served as a general in the Mexican War and refused to take a strong position on the slavery issue. He was elected in part because the Democrats' support for the 1850 Compromise was more clearly expressed, and many voters believed that the Compromise would ensure peace.

Pierce entered office benefiting from a general prosperity and a boom in railroading that would soon unite the two coasts; however, he was forced to deal with the consequences of a disastrous action taken by a member of his own party. Stephen Douglas, a senator from Illinois, helped draft and then force through a bill known as the Kansas-Nebraska Act. Douglas supported the building of a railroad from Chicago to California. In an effort to organize the Western territories through which the railroad would pass, Douglas's bill proposed that the residents of these territories would decide the question of whether or not slavery would be allowed, essentially **repealing** the Missouri Compromise. As a result, anti- and proslavery settlers rushed into Kansas, and violence followed.

Despite public outcry, Pierce signed the Kansas-Nebraska Act, further propelling the nation toward the Civil War. Many Democrats, disgusted by this action, left the party. Some, who claimed to be the ones who truly believed in Jefferson's principles of individual freedom, helped to launch a new party, one that they called "Republican" in honor of Jefferson's original party. This group formed the roots of what would become the modern Republican Party.

For their 1856 convention, the Democrats gathered in Cincinnati. The platform endorsed the Kansas-Nebraska Act as a "sound and safe solution of the 'slavery question,'" but Pierce was not renominated. The party instead turned to James Buchanan, who had served as Pierce's minister to Great Britain. His time out of the country contributed to his appeal. He had not been in the United States and so had not been involved in some of the most hostile fights of the past few years.

Buchanan's philosophy was that the decision about slavery belonged to the Constitution and to the Supreme Court. The bitterness over slavery had become too great for either side to accept a policy that favored the opposing position, however. Buchanan further added to the crisis when he suggested that Kansas be admitted to the Union as a slave state, angering Northerners, members of his own party, and the newly formed Republican Party. Kansas remained a territory, and Republicans gained a majority in the House in the midterm elections of 1858. Northern and Southern senators argued over bills. The country was dividing, and Buchanan lacked the skill or understanding to hold it together. He could not, in fact, even hold his own party together.

Franklin Pierce was the Democratic candidate for the election of 1852. He won by a landslide, 254 electoral votes to 42, against the Whig Party candidate.

THE DEMOCRATIC PARTY

A Divided Convention

In April 1860, the Democratic convention was held in Charleston, South Carolina, a friendly gesture toward the South to prevent the party from splitting. The gesture would prove unsuccessful. The Northern Democrats pushed

HON. STEPHEN A. DOUGLAS,

The leading Democratic candidate for the Presidency in 1860—Stephen Douglas.

hard for Stephen Douglas as their candidate. A group of Southern Democrats declared that they would leave the party unless its platform promised to guarantee slavery in the American territories. Douglas and his supporters bitterly opposed this, insisting instead that the subject of slavery should be voted on in each of the territories.

When the Southern Democrats failed to obtain the promise they wanted, many of them (including the entire delegation from Alabama) walked out of the convention. Douglas failed to gather the majority he needed, and the decision was made to hold a second convention in Baltimore.

The Baltimore meeting was every bit as disastrous as the one in Charleston. The acrimony between delegates from the North and the South continued. As a particularly bad omen, the floor of the convention hall collapsed during the meeting, forcing delegates to rush from the hall and stay away until the floor could be repaired. Douglas supporters refused to allow the delegates from Alabama and Louisiana (many of whom had walked out on the earlier meeting) to participate in the new meeting, prompting yet another walkout by delegates from many Southern states, including Virginia, as well as those from California and Oregon. When the meeting finally ended, Douglas was chosen as the nominee.

The battle was not yet over. The Southern Democrats who had walked out at the meeting held their own convention in Charleston. They took the name "National Democrats" and chose as their nominee Vice President John Breckinridge of Kentucky, with Senator Joseph Lane as his running mate. Their platform focused on protecting slavery. With the Democratic Party running two separate candidates and essentially two separate campaigns—one in the North and one in the South—it is not surprising that the newly formed Republican Party was successful and that its candidate, Abraham Lincoln, came to occupy the White House. At the end of the election, the Democratic Party was bitterly divided, foreshadowing the sharp division that would soon lead to the Civil War.

Text-Dependent Questions

1. What was James Polk's focus issue as president?

2. What was the Free Soil Party, and what did its members stand for?

3. Which president signed the Kansas-Nebraska Act, and why was it so disastrous for the country?

Research Project

Research one of the governmental orders referenced in this chapter, including the 1850 Compromise, the Fugitive Slave Law, and the Kansas-Nebraska Act. Write a brief report summarizing the bill, act, or law, including its key points, prominent voices in support of and opposition to it, and its impact on American history.

War and Politics

Words to Understand

Armistice: A formal declaration between parties to end a war.

Gold standard: A monetary system where the value of currency is based on a specific quantity of gold.

Tariff: A tax on imported or exported goods between nations.

Shortly after Lincoln's inauguration, war broke out between the North and the South. Lincoln's party changed its name from the Republican Party to the National Union Party, and many Democrats joined it in a show of support for the war effort. Others opposed the war and felt that the South should be allowed to secede. These so-called "Peace Democrats" were labeled "Copperheads" by their opponents, who accused them of behaving like snakes.

Lincoln was grateful for the support of the Democrats, and when he sought reelection in 1864, he chose as his vice president a former Democrat, Andrew Johnson of Tennessee. The Democrats chose a Union general, George McClellan, as their nominee. McClellan's platform argued for a negotiated settlement with the South, but the presence of many Democrats in Lincoln's National Union Party helped to ensure Lincoln's reelection.

Johnson became president when Lincoln was assassinated. His administration was tarnished by scandal, though, and when he sought

President Lincoln at his first inauguration in Washington, D.C., in 1861.

THE COPPERHEAD PARTY.— IN FAVOR OF A VIGOROUS PROSECUTION OF PEACE!

Democrats who opposed the war between North and South were labeled "Copperheads" by their opponents. In the cartoon above, the woman, Columbia (a poetic name for America), holds a shield labeled "Union" in order to defend herself from the caricatured Copperheads.

election in his own right, he faced both Republican opponents and a fierce challenge from the Democrats. He failed to win his party's nomination. Instead, it went to General Ulysses S. Grant. The Civil War had ended, and Democrats used racial prejudice as a way to frighten voters. They charged that Republican policies for rebuilding the South were intended to elevate former slaves above whites. Ultimately, the Democrats lost the election once again.

The Democrats failed to win the White House for 24 years. It was clear that the party needed new leadership and a new sense of direction. Not until 1884, with the nomination of Grover Cleveland, the former mayor of Buffalo and governor of New York, did the Democratic Party began to recover.

The party began an intensive campaign to restructure and reorganize. Workers were recruited not only at the national level but also at the state, county, and local levels. Cities were the focus of much of this recruiting, and newly arrived Irish and Central European working-class immigrants were specifically targeted. Party workers would provide these immigrants with much-needed services (such as helping them find jobs or arranging health care) in exchange for their votes.

Cleveland benefited from these efforts. He had worked hard to fight corruption, reform government, and reduce taxes. He and his Republican challenger, James Blaine, fought a bitter campaign, with scandals and gossip published to attack both sides. It was a close election, but Cleveland's New York electoral votes helped put him over the top.

Cleveland's two terms in office (one that began in 1884 and one eight years later) would be the only times a Democrat served as president in a period of 52 years. From 1860 to 1912, the Republicans would hold on to the White House with only those two exceptions.

The Democrats failed to elect a president for 24 years after the Civil War, until Grover Cleveland was nominated in 1884. Above is a campaign illustration showing Cleveland and his running mate, A. G. Thurman.

Cleveland was nominated for a second term, but he failed to win the election against the Republican candidate, Benjamin Harrison. Cleveland won the popular vote but not the electoral vote. The issue that had proved decisive involved **tariffs** (taxes) on imported goods. Cleveland challenged Harrison again in 1892, and this time he was up against a president weakened by poor financial management of the White House. Cleveland was elected, becoming the only president to serve two non-consecutive terms.

Cleveland may have regretted his decision to return to the White House. Within two months of beginning his second term, the stock market collapsed. Banks and railroads began to fail, and thousands of businesses were forced to declare bankruptcy.

Cleveland stubbornly clung to his economic policies, even as Americans lost their jobs and pleaded for relief. The Cleveland administration's failures sparked further division in the Democratic Party. Once split into Northern and Southern wings, now disagreements separated residents of the Northeast from people living in the South and the West. Democrats who represented farm regions and those from industrial areas disagreed on policy, including whether the American monetary system should be based on a gold or silver standard. Depression, strikes, and divisions in the party made it clear that a Democrat would not occupy the White House after Cleveland.

Cross of Gold

In the presidential elections of 1896, 1900, and 1908, the Democratic nominee was William Jennings Bryan, a congressman from Nebraska. Bryan strongly supported an American money system based on silver rather than gold—a popular position in the West, where silver was mined.

In 1896, the debate over a silver standard versus a **gold standard** occupied the Democratic Party convention. Bryan delivered one of the most famous speeches in political history, arguing that the Democratic Party must stand on the side of rural Americans, of the "struggling masses." His speech ended with the dramatic words, "You shall not press down upon the brow of labor this crown of thorns; you shall not crucify mankind upon a cross of gold."

The speech made Bryan famous, and it brought him the nomination that year and in 1900 and 1908. Bryan would fail to win the presidency, losing to William

President Grover Cleveland addresses the nation at his first presidential inauguration in 1885.

McKinley in 1896 and 1900 and to William Taft in 1908. Still, Bryan's candidacy changed the image of the Democratic Party, shaping it once again into the party of the people.

Sixteen years passed without a Democrat in the White House, and that trend might have continued had it not been for division within the Republican Party. Republican President William Taft sought reelection in 1912, but his former friend and supporter, and former president, Theodore Roosevelt, decided to challenge Taft for the nomination. When he failed to win the Republican nomination, Roosevelt left the party and formed his own, the Progressive, or "Bull Moose," Party. This split in the Republicans was a boost to the Democratic Party and its candidate, Woodrow Wilson.

Wilson had only limited experience in politics and none at all at the national level. He had served as the president of Princeton University and had only recently won his first political election to become the governor of New Jersey. Wilson's campaign focused on what he called a plan for "New Freedom," which involved breaking up excessive power in the hands of big businesses in order to ensure protection

Woodrow Wilson at work.

for small businesses and farms to compete in the marketplace. Wilson campaigned feverishly, traveling by train from one small town to another and often making several stops and speeches a day. His pitch for the Democratic Party as a progressive party and the split between the Republicans brought enough votes for Wilson to become president.

As president, Wilson also took on the leadership of the Democratic Party. He was determined to focus on his "New Freedom" agenda, and, when World War I broke out in Europe, he first stated that the United States would remain neutral in the conflict. Wilson helped to champion several progressive laws, including those to ban child labor. His successes and the fact that the country was not at war helped win him reelection in 1920. Soon, however, the sinking of three American merchant ships by German forces made it impossible for Wilson to keep his promise of neutrality. He continued to work for peace while preparing the country's military. When the war finally ended, Wilson insisted on attending the peace conference held in Paris, making him the first American president to go abroad on a diplomatic mission. There, he signed the Treaty of Versailles, the peace settlement following the **armistice** that ended World War I.

This treaty also founded an international organization called the League of Nations. This was Wilson's brainchild, a forum that he felt would serve to preserve the peace for future generations. But the U.S. Senate did not ratify the treaty, and the United States never joined the League, leaving Wilson embarrassed and defeated.

Wilson kept his promise to support the right for women to vote, and the constitutional amendment finally was ratified in August 1920, in time for women to vote in the presidential election.

WILSON'S FOURTEEN POINTS

In a speech given on January 8, 1918, President Woodrow Wilson outlined his precepts for world peace and the end of World War I in a statement known as the Fourteen Points. The Fourteen Points were progressive in their outlook, with statements on transparency in government, reduction in weapons and armed forces worldwide, and the formation of a "League of Nations" that would work together on behalf of world peace. Some foreign leaders wondered whether Wilson's view was too idealistic. Although the Fourteen Points helped to end World War I, they were ultimately superseded by the much harsher Treaty of Versailles. Still, Wilson was awarded the Nobel Peace Prize for his efforts in 1919.

Still, the party failed to hold onto the presidency: Warren G. Harding easily defeated the Democratic nominee, Governor James Cox of Ohio, and his running mate, Assistant Secretary of the Navy Franklin Roosevelt.

Franklin Roosevelt began to work behind the scenes to help ensure reform of the Democratic Party. His belief was that the party was simply reacting to events in the Republican administration, hoping that the Republicans would make mistakes. Instead, he urged, the party needed to become more proactive, creating policies and shaping an agenda rather than responding to Republican policies.

In 1928, Roosevelt was elected governor of New York, launching him on the path that would lead to the White House. That path was made easier by the disastrous policies of Herbert Hoover, who was elected president in 1928, just before the nation's economy collapsed into the Great Depression. As Americans lost their jobs and their homes, Hoover continued to insist that relief should come at the local, not the national, level.

The 1912 split in the Republican Party was a boon for the Democratic Party, which had not elected a president for 16 years. Woodrow Wilson, pictured above, promoted the Democratic Party as progressive. Here, Wilson throws the first pitch on opening day in 1916.

In New York, Governor Roosevelt created numerous programs to respond to the Depression, providing relief for the unemployed and focusing on plans for public works projects. Roosevelt's successful programs in New York won him the Democratic nomination in 1932.

Despite being in a wheelchair, Roosevelt campaigned vigorously and energetically, reassuring voters that the country needed to be rebuilt from the bottom up and that he would stand as the candidate for the "forgotten man." At the Democratic convention, Roosevelt broke with the tradition of having candidates nominated in their absence. Instead, he took a small plane from Albany to Chicago (another noteworthy deed in those early days of flying, portraying him as a man of action) and arrived at the convention to accept the Democratic nomination in person.

Facing a country in economic crisis, President Hoover warned that Roosevelt's plans were not specific and lacked substance. The nation was desperate for change, however, and, on March 4, 1933, Franklin Delano Roosevelt became the 32nd president of the United States.

Roosevelt's presidency would mark a dramatic turning point in the country's leadership and in the fortunes of the Democratic Party. Through dynamic leadership and creative policymaking, Roosevelt would win election to four terms as president and ensure that the White House remained in Democratic hands for 20 years.

Text-Dependent Questions

1. What was Grover Cleveland's political experience before becoming president?

2. Who was Williams Jennings Bryan, and what was the subject of the speech that brought him the presidential nomination in 1896?

3. What was the key difference between Herbert Hoover's and Franklin Roosevelt's responses to the Depression?

Research Project

Research Woodrow Wilson's role in the planning and creation of the League of Nations. Find out about the goals of the League, its key members, some of its notable accomplishments, and reasons for its eventual dissolution. Write a summary of your findings, including reasons why the United States never formally joined the League.

A New Deal

Words to Understand

Bias: Favoring a particular person, idea, or group in a way that can be seen as unfair.

Desegregate: To end a practice of racial separation.

Polling: In politics, soliciting the opinions of the public to help determine electoral preferences.

During his inaugural speech, Franklin Roosevelt told the nation, "The only thing we have to fear is fear itself." His smiling face and take-charge manner demonstrated that he had confidence in his ability to help America rebuild after the crippling Depression.

Roosevelt's decisiveness was evident from the moment he assumed the presidency. Immediately after his inaugural parade, he had his cabinet sworn in all at the same time. He declared a four-day bank holiday and called a special session of Congress to create emergency banking legislation. A few days later, he spoke to the nation on the radio, using a format he would make famous: the "fireside chat." He explained to everyone what he had done during the bank holiday and what he planned to do in the near future, asking Americans to return their savings to the banks when they reopened.

During Roosevelt's first 100 days in office, he sent to Congress a series of emergency bills intended to address the country's economic crisis.

Herbert Hoover (left) and Franklin D. Roosevelt (right) en route to Roosevelt's inauguration in 1933.

President Franklin D. Roosevelt addresses the nation about the progress of the war in one of his famous fireside chats. Roosevelt introduced his radio talks to explain administration policies and to appeal to the people for support during the difficult 1930s. News outlets would set up cameras and microphones to record the president as he spoke.

THE DEMOCRATIC PARTY

Some of the bills focused on jobless relief to the states, others on cutbacks for government spending. There were bills to create the Civilian Conservation Corps and the Tennessee Valley Authority and others to protect home mortgages and reform railroads. Roosevelt spoke to the American public using his radio fireside chats to explain what he was doing, creating an atmosphere of confidence at a time when many were still out of work and worried about the future.

Roosevelt's successes gave the Democratic Party an opportunity to follow his model. Roosevelt's programs, called the "New Deal," also gave his party a new chance to identify itself as a party of optimism and change. He sponsored programs for better working conditions and supported union organizing, which resulted in strong union and worker support for the Democratic Party when Roosevelt sought reelection in 1936. It was in this campaign that political **polling** first became an important part of the election process. The Democratic Party surveyed voters not only on their choice for president but also on their views of Roosevelt's programs and policies. They could then use that information to target voters on the issues that mattered to them and to design better radio ads.

With this election, more voters identified themselves as supporters of the Democratic Party than ever before. For the first time, the Democratic Party was able to claim solid support from African Americans (a significant change—previously, they had supported the Republican Party of Abraham Lincoln) and from farmers; both groups felt that they had benefited from legislation championed by Roosevelt. The Democrats also profited from the support of unions, the unemployed (who believed that Roosevelt's policies would help them soon), and immigrants.

Roosevelt won reelection, but his plan to reorganize the Supreme Court prompted conservatives within his own party to protest. By 1940, Hitler's army was on the march and Europe was enmeshed in war. Roosevelt decided that the global events made it critical for the United States to have an experienced leader, despite the fact that no American president had served more than two terms. Roosevelt made it clear to leading Democrats that he would accept the party's nomination for a third term if it were offered to him. It was.

Roosevelt told the nation that he needed to remain at the White House rather than spend time in political debates. His Republican opponent, Wendell Wilkie, took advantage of Roosevelt's absence on the campaign trail by crisscrossing the country, outlining his vision for the future. Wilkie had once been a Democrat himself—in fact, he had voted for Roosevelt in 1932. Wilkie's campaign suggested that Roosevelt was trying to create a monarchy in America, with Roosevelt as its king.

Roosevelt reassured the American public that "your boys are not going to be sent into foreign wars," a promise he claimed to have kept after the United States entered World War II. The Japanese attack on Pearl Harbor was an attack on U.S. soil, he reasoned, meaning that the war could not be described as "foreign."

Roosevelt won a decisive victory over Wilkie. Less than a year after he began his third term, the United States entered World War II. Gradually, the war began to turn in the favor of the United States and its allies, and by 1944 Roosevelt's image as a confident commander in chief made it possible for him to consider a fourth term as president.

PARTY PLANNING

After the 1940 campaign, Wilkie and Roosevelt mended their relationship and discussed an interesting possibility. Both the Republican and Democratic parties had conservatives who had more in common with each other than with more liberal members. Both men were frustrated by the conservative members of their respective parties—particularly by their unwillingness to consider change. The men discussed a dramatic proposal: to completely remake the Democratic and Republican parties into two new political parties, one conservative and one liberal. The two men apparently hoped that their new party system might be put into place by 1948. By 1948, however, both Wilkie and Roosevelt were dead. In the following decades, the parties would eventually shift, with the Republican Party becoming the party of conservatives and the Democratic Party attracting liberals.

Harry Truman

When running for his fourth term as president in 1944, Roosevelt decided to change his vice president. Roosevelt chose Senator Harry S. Truman of Missouri as his running mate. With a modest amount of campaigning, Roosevelt defeated his Republican opponent, Thomas Dewey.

Within six months of taking office for the fourth time, Roosevelt was dead, having suffered a cerebral hemorrhage. Truman became president. Truman faced the challenge of filling the shoes of the man who had occupied the Oval Office longer than any other and who had dramatically reshaped the Democratic Party and its policies. The party for which Truman was now the symbol was focused on new and challenging issues, many of which would occupy it for most of the century—civil rights, foreign policy, and the expanding role of the federal government. It was becoming a party concentrated in Northern cities and dependent on the support of immigrants and labor, as well as that of African American voters.

Truman made the difficult decision to use the atomic bomb on Japan to bring an end to World War II. In the years immediately after the war, conflict with the Soviet Union led to concern about the possible spread of Communism, and the American economy faltered. Truman faced opposition within his party, and Republicans saw real opportunity to recapture the White House after 16 years. They again chose Thomas Dewey of New York as their presidential candidate.

The election of 1948 was the first time presidential party conventions were televised. The audiences were generally small, and events were not planned to coincide with television coverage in the way that speeches and events today are scheduled to play during prime-time hours. Certain members of the Democratic Party made an appeal to General Dwight Eisenhower, the leader of the Allied troops in Europe, to challenge Truman for the nomination, but Eisenhower refused.

This cleared the way for Truman to be nominated. Civil rights became a major issue for the party platform. At the convention, the mayor of Minneapolis, Hubert Humphrey, who was at the time in a race for the Senate to represent Minnesota, made a speech that urged Democrats to "get out of the shadow of states' rights and walk forthrightly into the bright sunshine of human rights."

Harry Truman and civil rights.

Dixiecrats

There were many, particularly Southern, delegates within the Democratic Party who disagreed with this commitment to civil rights and with Truman's executive order to **desegregate** the armed forces. Some left the party, gathered in Birmingham, Alabama, and nominated their own candidate for president, Governor Strom Thurmond of

When President Roosevelt died in 1944, Harry S. Truman, his vice president, took over. Truman inherited leadership of a radically reshaped Democratic Party. In 1945, Truman announced Japan's surrender and the end of World War II. Though some in his own party opposed him, he was reelected to the presidency in 1948.

South Carolina, on the "States' Rights Democratic Party" ticket. These "States' Rights Democrats" (also known as Dixiecrats) supported a platform based on racial segregation. The Dixiecrats were able to have their ticket declared the official Democratic ticket in Alabama, Louisiana, Mississippi, and South Carolina, and ultimately won in these four states.

Early polls predicted that Dewey would be the winner, but Truman pulled off an upset and managed to retain the presidency for the Democrats. The Dixiecrats disappeared as a separate political party, but their impact was clear. Disillusioned with the Democratic Party and its position on civil rights, many Dixiecrats would eventually join the Republican Party, including the man who ran for the presidency on the States' Rights Democratic Party ticket, Strom Thurmond.

A Fair Deal

In his inaugural speech, Truman described the role of his administration: to ensure that Americans were given a "fair deal." A twist on Roosevelt's "New Deal," the "Fair Deal" promised new action in civil rights, government aid to public education, and national health insurance. Truman's Fair Deal also requested higher social security payments and an increase in the minimum wage.

Truman had hoped to focus on domestic policy in this new term, but events in the world soon made that impossible. Tensions with the Soviet Union raised fears of Communist influence throughout the world. When North Korea invaded South Korea, the president ordered U.S. troops into the conflict as part of a United Nations force.

Truman himself decided that nearly eight years in office were enough. In a campaign in which primaries were becoming increasingly important (1952), Truman urged support for the Democratic candidate he liked best—Governor Adlai Stevenson of Illinois. Stevenson was witty and articulate, but he was little match for his popular opponent, Republican Dwight Eisenhower, the general whom Democrats had hoped to draft as their nominee only a few years earlier. This was the first presidential campaign in which paid television advertising played an important role; the ads for Eisenhower proclaimed, "I like Ike," whereas Stevenson seemed too intellectual to many voters. Republicans effectively labeled Democrats the party of "Korea, Communism, and Corruption," bringing an end to 20 years of Democratic administrations.

Winds of Change

The next eight years represented a time of transition and change within the Democratic Party. Eisenhower suffered a heart attack near the end of his first term. His vice president, Richard Nixon, was unpopular, and the Democrats hoped that the possibility of his becoming president if Eisenhower's health were to fail might win voters who wanted to prevent that. Eisenhower recovered, however, and Adlai Stevenson (once again the Democratic candidate) failed to take a significant number of votes from the popular president in 1956.

By 1960, a new candidate had emerged to challenge the Republican candidate, Vice President Nixon, for the presidency. John F. Kennedy, a senator from Massachusetts, had given a stirring speech at the 1956 Democratic convention and was the kind of handsome and charismatic candidate the party needed. Kennedy's candidacy faced some challenges: He was young (if elected, he would be only 43 years old at his inauguration) and he was Catholic. No Catholic had ever been elected president, and the religious **bias** of that time forced Kennedy to make it clear that he would make policy based on what was best for the United States, not what was best for the Catholic Church.

As his running mate, Kennedy chose a man who had opposed him for the Democratic nomination: Speaker of the House Lyndon B. Johnson of Texas. Kennedy had offered Johnson the nomination as a courtesy and was somewhat shocked when he accepted.

The contrast between the Republican and Democratic parties was dramatically illustrated by their respective candidates in 1960. Richard Nixon, the vice president, had built his conservative reputation on his deep suspicion of Communists and his willingness to serve as Eisenhower's attack dog during their campaigns. In a campaign speech, Nixon had foolishly promised to visit all 50 states, a pledge that would force him into an exhausting series of campaign appearances while Kennedy was free to focus on the states that were most critical to his victory.

During the campaign, Kennedy learned that civil rights leader Martin Luther King Jr. had been arrested in Georgia and sentenced to four months of hard labor. He telephoned King's wife to ask what he could do to help. The call and the pressure that Kennedy then put on Georgia authorities to release King prompted strong support for Kennedy among African Americans.

A series of televised debates played a critical role in the 1960 election. Kennedy was tanned and rested and appeared relaxed and confident on camera. Nixon, on the other hand, seemed uncomfortable, and his sweat was visible to the television audience. The election was close, but in the end Kennedy won, giving the Democrats the go-ahead to set out toward what Kennedy had described as the "New Frontier."

A New Era

Kennedy began his presidency with confidence and enthusiasm, and the country quickly rallied behind the president and his glamorous young wife. The Kennedys'

Richard Nixon (right) and John F. Kennedy (left) are shown in a photograph from one of the 1960 presidential campaign debates. The televised debates strongly influenced the election. Kennedy's youthful, handsome appearance was particularly appealing to voters.

young children roamed through the White House. Kennedy brought with him a staff of well-educated, committed young men and women dedicated to public service.

Kennedy urged support for the U.S. space program and, less successfully, for civil rights. He also launched the Peace Corps. When the Soviets placed missiles in nearby Cuba, Kennedy made it clear that the situation would not be accepted. The Soviets were finally forced to back down and remove the missiles. It was also during the Kennedy administration that the U.S. role in Vietnam began to widen, with what would prove to be disastrous consequences for future presidents. American troops were sent as "advisers" to the government in South Vietnam to assist in its efforts to resist Communist attacks from North Vietnam. Kennedy had indicated his interest in eventually pulling the troops out, planning to do it in his second term.

In November 1963, Kennedy traveled to Texas, in part to help settle a disagreement between two key members of the Democratic Party there, Governor

John Connally and U.S. Senator Ralph Yarborough. By publicly appearing around the state with both politicians, Kennedy hoped to heal their disagreement (at least publicly) and also to ensure Texas votes for his planned bid for reelection in 1964. On November 22, while traveling in a motorcade through Dallas, Kennedy was shot. He died shortly afterward.

Kennedy's vice president, Lyndon Johnson, faced the difficult task of filling the shoes of the popular leader who had brought glamour to the White House and inspiration to many young voters. Johnson made it clear from the beginning that he intended to continue Kennedy's legacy. From this promise, the so-called Great Society was born.

President John F. Kennedy and his wife moments before his assassination in Dallas, Texas.

THE DEMOCRATIC PARTY

Text-Dependent Questions

1. What global events prompted Franklin Roosevelt to seek a third term in 1940?

2. Name two proposals of Harry Truman's "Fair Deal."

3. What were some challenges John F. Kennedy's candidacy faced in 1960?

Research Project

Research one of the public works relief agencies created by Franklin Roosevelt's New Deal, including the Civilian Conservation Corps, the Tennessee Valley Authority, or the Works Progress Association. Look at its history, its particular focus and goals, some of its notable accomplishments, administrators, and alumni, and other pertinent information. Write a summary of your findings.

Changing Society and the Modern Democratic Party

Johnson was committed to continuing the plans set out by Kennedy during his presidency. He quickly shepherded a tax cut and a civil rights bill to bar discrimination in public accommodations. He outlined his plans for a "Great Society" in which opportunity would be shared by all Americans. He also announced the launch of a "War on Poverty" and championed the Job Corps for school dropouts and Head Start for pre-school children.

The war on Vietnam took some of Johnson's focus away from his domestic programs, however. The situation in South Korea was increasingly unstable, and rather than following Kennedy's plan for a troop withdrawal, Johnson increased the number of attacks against North Vietnam.

President Lyndon B. Johnson's official portrait.

After President John F. Kennedy was assassinated, his vice president, Lyndon B. Johnson (above), assumed the presidency. Just two hours and eight minutes after Kennedy's assassination, Johnson was sworn in aboard Air Force One at Love Field in Dallas, Texas. He continued Kennedy's programs and was reelected in 1964.

Johnson ran as the Democratic nominee for the presidency in 1964. His opponent was Senator Barry Goldwater, known for his outspoken anti-Communist views and his adversarial position toward China and Russia. Playing on fears that Goldwater might launch a nuclear war with one of the two Communist nations, Johnson spoke of working toward easing tensions with the Soviet Union. Television commercials for the Democratic candidate emphasized him as the candidate working for peace. He won a commanding victory.

With Democratic control of both the House and Senate, Johnson was able to push through even more legislation to help shape the "Great Society," including

Medicare, aid to secondary and higher education, low-income housing, and a new Voting Rights Act.

America was at a crossroads, though, and the great society that Johnson dreamed of would soon confront the reality of an increasingly militant and violent population. A march to register voters in Alabama led by Martin Luther King Jr. was attacked by state troopers in Selma. Race riots erupted in cities, and the war in Vietnam continued to kill Americans and spark protests, many of them on college campuses. It was increasingly difficult for President Johnson to travel anywhere without tight security.

In 1968, Senator Eugene McCarthy of Minnesota announced his intention to challenge the president for the Democratic nomination. McCarthy's antiwar position appealed to young voters, who rallied behind his cause. In the first primary, in New Hampshire, McCarthy won nearly as many votes as the president. After McCarthy's successful challenge, Senator Robert Kennedy of Massachusetts, brother of the former president, also decided to seek the Democratic nomination.

On March 31, 1968, Johnson went on television to deliver a speech about the Vietnam War. He spoke for nearly 45 minutes about the recent bombing of North Vietnam, his decision to send 13,500 more American troops over the next five months, and the funds that would be spent to equip South Vietnamese troops. Then, without advance warning, Johnson concluded his speech with the shocking announcement that he would not seek another term as president.

Turmoil in the Party

Johnson's announcement threw the party into chaos. Four days later, Martin Luther King Jr. was assassinated. His murder was followed by riots in more than 100 cities.

Johnson's vice president, Hubert Humphrey, now decided to seek the Democratic nomination. The three candidates—McCarthy, Kennedy, and Humphrey—struggled to position themselves on the issues. Humphrey faced the most difficult challenge: He inherited the problems of the Johnson administration and was unable to distance himself from Johnson's policies without appearing disloyal. Robert Kennedy won the critical California primary, but as he made his way to the press conference after his victory, he was shot and killed.

The Democratic Party convention, held in Chicago in 1968, would go down in history as one of the most violent and chaotic political conventions ever held. Chicago's mayor, Richard Daley, had ordered the convention center surrounded by barbed wire and a chain-link fence. City police and members of the Illinois National Guard scrutinized the delegates as they entered the convention. This did not stop the protestors from gathering outside and clashing with police, who responded by clubbing protestors and throwing them into police vans. Inside, the atmosphere was every bit as fierce. Supporters of McCarthy chanted, "Stop the war!" and insisted that the Democratic platform contain a clause that called for an immediate end to the bombing in North Vietnam and a negotiated withdrawal of all American troops.

The convention proved to be a boon to the Republicans and their candidate, former vice president Richard Nixon. Images of the violence of the Democratic

The 1968 Democratic convention became notorious for the demonstrations, both inside and out, that disrupted business. Above, police and demonstrators clash at Grant Park in Chicago, where the convention was held.

convention, the race riots, and the war protests helped Nixon's campaign as a "law and order" candidate who would return the country to the peace of the Eisenhower years. This was enough for Nixon to win the White House, although he inherited many of the problems that had plagued his Democratic predecessor.

The 1970s

The country was sharply divided into young and old, liberal and conservative, anti-war and anti-Communist. By 1971, George McGovern, a senator from South Dakota, had announced his decision to seek the Democratic Party nomination. He was one of many Democrats who sought the nomination.

Shortly before the New York primary, a break-in was reported at the Democratic National Committee's headquarters in the Watergate building complex in Washington, D.C. Police caught five men attempting to burglarize the office of the Democratic Party chairman, and it was soon learned that the five were all connected to the Republican Committee for the Re-election of the President. Nixon and his aides denied any connection or involvement. Their statements were proved false—after the election.

McGovern won the Democratic nomination, thanks in large part to his anti-war platform. Nixon effectively portrayed the Democrats as a party of "long-haired" liberals who would weaken America militarily and in the eyes of the world. Nixon also stressed that peace was "at hand." He won every state except Massachusetts. The victory proved short-lived, however. Vice President Spiro Agnew was forced to resign when it was learned that he had accepted payoffs from Maryland contractors and evaded income tax payments. House Minority Leader Gerald Ford was named the new vice president.

In February 1974, the House Judiciary Committee began an investigation into Nixon's involvement with Watergate. Evidence on secretly recorded tapes made it clear that the president had been involved in the break-in and in the cover-up that followed. Nixon learned he was likely to face impeachment, and he decided to resign.

Ford took office promising change and a clean slate. His support quickly disappeared when, one month after becoming president, he issued a complete pardon for Nixon. He made the decision to spare the country the turmoil of seeing its former president on trial, but it doomed Ford's chances to win the presidency in 1976.

The issues that dominated the 1976 presidential race were integrity and character. A number of candidates vied for the Democratic nomination, and Governor Jimmy Carter of Georgia succeeded. His campaign focused on his status as a Washington outsider, a man of honor and character, a graduate of the naval academy, and a hard-working farmer—the first farmer to seek the presidency since Jefferson, according to some campaign ads. Carter positioned himself as a "**centrist**," with policies and ideas that straddled the line between liberal and conservative. He promised in his campaign never to lie to the American people.

The election was close, but the Democrats won, taking back the White House after eight years of Republican domination.

Four Troubled Years

Carter took office with the promise of a fresh start and a government that could be trusted; however, his four years in office were marked by poor decisions and mismanagement. Carter's status as an outsider made it difficult for him to form the kind of alliances that help bills pass through Congress and to ensure that an agenda can be carried out.

Carter had no foreign policy experience, making it even more difficult for him to assess and respond to events around the world. Efforts to negotiate an arms-control treaty with the Soviet Union failed. He did successfully negotiate a Middle East peace treaty between Israel and Egypt, but the U.S. economy faltered, and the country was beset by an energy crisis, with Americans forced to wait in long lines at gas stations simply to put gasoline in their cars.

A revolution in Iran would prove to be the most decisive blow to Carter's presidency. When the ruler of Iran, the Shah, was forced out of the country after a revolution that ushered in a fundamentalist Islamic regime, he asked to be allowed into the United States to seek medical treatment. Carter's decision to admit the Shah triggered the seizure of the American embassy in Iran's capital, Tehran, and the capture of 66 Americans as hostages. A failed attempt to rescue the hostages

A speech on the Iran hostage crisis.

In 1976, Jimmy Carter took the White House with promises of a fresh start and a govern-ment that could be trusted. Ultimately, however, his presidency was doomed by numerous crises, including an energy shortage and Americans held hostage in Iran.

Changing Society and the Modern Democratic Party

ended in disaster, conveying to Americans an image of their country as incompetent and helpless, even to protect its own citizens.

Carter received the nomination of the Democratic Party when he sought reelection. He was challenged by a former actor and governor of California, Ronald Reagan, whose Republican campaign highlighted Carter's mistakes and promised a return to a strong America.

As the hostage crisis dragged on for month after month, with efforts at negotiating their release proving futile, Carter's popularity began to drop in the polls. The Republican campaign effectively targeted the Democratic president by posing the question, "Are you better off than you were four years ago?" For most Americans, the answer was "No."

Jimmy Carter became the first Democratic incumbent to lose a bid for reelection since Grover Cleveland in 1888. The Iranians released the hostages shortly after Ronald Reagan's inauguration, a final blow to the Democratic president.

The 1980 election marked a fundamental shift in American politics. Ronald Reagan and the Republicans had accurately read the sentiment of many Americans: They wanted a more conservative government. With what came to be known as the "Reagan Revolution," a new era began, one in which many of the policies launched by Democratic presidents like Roosevelt and Johnson would be abandoned gradually.

Reagan, Bush, and the Rise of the 'New Democrats'

Reagan occupied the White House for eight years. His policies—cutting taxes and reducing many federal programs that helped the poor and unemployed while increasing military spending—served to jump-start the economy.

In 1984, Jimmy Carter's vice president, Walter Mondale, ran as the Democratic challenger to the incumbent Reagan. Mondale failed to capture voters' support, even with his choice of running mate, Geraldine Ferraro—the first female vice-presidential candidate for a major party. In 1988, Massachusetts Governor Michael Dukakis also failed in his effort to recapture the White House for the Democrats. Defining himself as the heir to the Reagan tradition, Vice President George H.W. Bush won a decisive victory.

In 1984, the Democrats nominated Walter Mondale. His running mate, Geraldine Ferraro, was the first female vice-presidential candidate for a major party. Above, Ferraro (right) and Mondale (left) wave to the crowd at a campaign event.

The Democrats had failed in three consecutive elections. Their traditional programs, based on support for the disadvantaged and the needy, had proved unsuccessful. It was clear that the Democratic Party needed to redefine itself, and its candidates, if it were ever to recapture the White House.

In 1991, President George H.W. Bush oversaw a successful effort to force Iraqi leader Saddam Hussein out of nearby Kuwait in a military campaign known as Operation Desert Storm. After the victory, Bush's approval ratings soared to nearly 90 percent. He seemed unbeatable, and many wary Democratic candidates who had been considering a run for the White House decided to postpone their efforts until after the 1992 election.

In the midst of this, Governor Bill Clinton of Arkansas won the 1992 Democratic Party nomination. Clinton wisely chose to position himself as a centrist. As the campaign season began, the American economy began to falter, and the Clinton campaign focused on this issue. Signs at the Clinton campaign head-quarters reminded staffers, "It's the economy, stupid."

As his running mate, Clinton chose another young Southern Democrat—Al Gore of Tennessee. The two traveled around the country by bus, representing them-selves as a "new generation of Democrats" who called for an "end to welfare as we know it," support for the death penalty, and a rejection of "tax-and-spend politics." Suddenly, the Democrats were beginning to sound a lot like the Republicans.

In the end, Clinton won a slim majority of 43 percent of the votes. Even third-party candidate Ross Perot performed strongly, winning 19 percent of the popular vote. Clinton had succeeded in reshaping the Democratic Party to appeal to new voters, recognizing the desire for change while positioning himself as a "New Democrat."

The Comeback Kid

Clinton's first few months in office were marked by a series of embarrassing stum-bles. He failed to win support for his dramatic plan to reform health care and was forced to withdraw several early candidates for his cabinet when questions were raised about their backgrounds. Criticisms were made that Clinton, while claim-ing to be a "New Democrat," was secretly the same old liberal Democrat. Midterm elections brought a severe rebuke to the Clinton White House, as Republicans took control of both the House and the Senate.

Clinton wisely decided to shift back to the center, proposing what he called a "Middle Class Bill of Rights" that featured a middle-income tax cut. His policies focused not on an increased role for government (the traditional policy for Demo-cratic presidents) but instead on individuals, on what was described as "opportunity with responsibility." He proposed a balanced budget plan—this would ultimately lead to a showdown with House of Representatives Speaker Newt Gingrich, which resulted in a temporary shutdown of the federal government. As the 1996 election drew closer, Clinton declared, "The era of big government is over."

With a healthy economy and the Republicans successfully depicted as "extreme," Clinton won reelection. The Democratic platform had reflected Clinton's "New Democrat" focus, with plans for welfare legislation, deficit reduction, tougher anticrime bills, middle-class tax cuts, and a balanced budget.

Arkansas Governor Bill Clinton won the Democratic nomination for president in 1992. He won the election after positioning himself in the political center and focusing on the faltering American economy.

Clinton's second term began on a strong note. The economy was strong, and the United States was at peace. There were ongoing questions about Clinton's personal and financial conduct, however, which ultimately led to an investigation. The investigation suggested that Clinton had had an inappropriate relationship with a White House intern, a charge that Clinton at first denied and then was forced to acknowledge. On December 19th, 1998, the House voted to impeach Clinton on charges of **perjury** and obstruction of justice. The impeachment process then moved to the Senate for trial, where Clinton was acquitted of the charges.

For his remaining two years in office, Clinton focused on building his legacy, but the trial and the scandals uncovered by the investigation would haunt his presidency and set a bad precedent for Vice President Al Gore when he sought the presidency in 2000.

A Bitter Fight

The 2000 election focused almost exclusively on domestic issues—matters like prescription drug plans for senior citizens, social security, and education. Al Gore was challenged by Republican Governor George W. Bush of Texas, the son of former president George H.W. Bush. Learning from the successes of Clinton and the "New Democrats," both candidates positioned themselves at the center, avoiding the more extreme positions of members of their respective parties. George W. Bush campaigned as a "compassionate conservative," and Al Gore focused on his plans to strengthen education and protect the environment.

The election was the closest in American history, prompting a recount of votes in Florida that left the question of who would be the next president of the United States unanswered for 36 days. A controversial Supreme Court decision finally brought the recount to an end, and George W. Bush was declared the winner.

With the beginning of his presidency under a cloud, it seemed possible to many Democrats that Bush, like his father, would be a one-term president. Then the terrorist attacks on September 11, 2001, changed the political climate. Bush was able to rally the nation against those who had attacked it and to inspire Democrats to join with Republicans in his decision to attack those responsible—the al-Qaeda terrorist network, based in Afghanistan.

The president's decision to expand the war on terrorism into Iraq gradually eroded the bipartisan support he had enjoyed. The Bush administration presented evidence that suggested a possible link between al-Qaeda and Iraqi leader Saddam Hussein and charged Hussein with attempting to stockpile biological, chemical, and nuclear weapons.

The evidence of this connection would later prove faulty, however. Although a U.S.-led coalition of troops was able to defeat the Iraqi army quickly and ultimately capture Hussein, Iraq erupted in violence. Questions about the U.S. involvement in Iraq became central issues of the 2004 election, as Democratic Senator John Kerry of Massachusetts challenged President Bush in his bid for reelection. For the first time in many years, the election focused on terrorism and foreign policy, with the economy and other domestic issues playing minor roles.

In the 2004 election, the Democratic and Republican candidates returned, in a sense, to the positions that had defined their parties for many years. The Republican candidate, President Bush, focused on his role as the experienced, steady commander in chief, a leader equipped to handle a dangerous and uncertain world. Democratic Party candidate Kerry stressed his connection to the concerns of average Americans. Concerns about safety played a key role for many voters, though, and President Bush was able to win reelection.

Beyond the Bush Era

George W. Bush's second term was plagued by the wars he had launched in Iraq and Afghanistan. Fighting on both fronts continued with no end in sight (as of 2018 the war in Afghanistan was still ongoing, and there were over 5,000 troops still deployed to Iraq), leading to fatigue at home and escalating violence and chaos abroad.

STRONG AT HOME, RESPECTED IN THE WORLD

The 2004 Democratic National platform, titled "Strong at Home, Respected in the World," reflected concerns about America's safety after the September 11, 2001, attacks while promising a "new direction." The platform included a nod to the party's history:

... Our vision has deep roots in our Declaration of Independence and Franklin Delano Roosevelt's Four Freedoms, and in the tough-minded tradition of engagement and leadership—a tradition forged by Wilson and Roosevelt in two world wars, then championed by Truman and Kennedy during the Cold War. We believe in an America that people around the world admire, because they know we cherish not just our freedom, but theirs. Not just our democracy, but their hope for it. Not just our peace and security, but the world's. We believe in an America that cherishes freedom, safeguards our people, forges alliances, and commands respect. That is the America we are going to build. ...

Source: The Democratic Party. Available online. URL: http://www.democrats.org.

Questions in the press began to surface around the Bush administration's authorization of torture—which is prohibited by international human rights law and treatises including the Geneva Conventions—at military prisons including Guantanamo Bay in Cuba and Abu Ghraib in Iraq. Additionally, Bush's poor response to the devastation of Hurricane Katrina in Louisiana in 2005 and economic policies that led to a widespread financial crisis in 2008 caused his popularity levels to plummet.

The time was right for a Democratic takeover of the White House, and multiple candidates began campaigning for the party's nomination. By 2007, three leading candidates had emerged: Hilary Clinton, senator from New York and husband of former president Bill; John Edwards, a former senator from North Carolina and the 2004 vice-presidential candidate; and a young senator from Illinois named Barack Obama. Edwards suspended his campaign in January 2008 as Clinton and Obama pulled ahead.

The contest had historic pedigree before it even began: If nominated, Obama would be the first African American to represent a major party in the presidential election—and if victorious, the first African American to occupy the highest office in the land. Young voters were galvanized by his John F. Kennedy–like charisma, and the possibility of such dramatic change after eight years of the Bush administration excited many on the left.

Clinton stressed her political experience throughout the primary, painting Obama as untested and saying in one debate that his presidency would be "a roll of the dice." Clinton, however, was haunted by her vote to authorize the Iraq War in 2002, which was extremely unpopular among Democrats. Obama overcame a few campaign missteps—including comments at a San Francisco fundraiser that seemed insensitive to working-class voters—to gather momentum throughout 2008, including sweeping 11 contests in 11 days in February and winning key contests in North Carolina and Oregon later that spring. Clinton could not catch up, and on June 7th she formally ended her campaign and endorsed Obama.

The Obama Years

On August 27, 2008, the Democratic Party officially nominated Obama as the party's candidate for president. He defeated Republican John McCain, senator from Arizona, in the general election. Pundits cited his concern for the middle class, proposals for a more fair and equitable health care system, and selection of the steady, experienced Delaware Senator Joe Biden as a running mate (in contrast to McCain's selection of Alaska Governor Sarah Palin, whom many saw as woefully inexperienced).

With the nation's stain of slavery very much in the public memory, the election of the first African American president was a deeply symbolic turning point in American history. Obama would go on to serve two terms, defeating former Massachusetts governor Mitt Romney in 2012. His eight-year tenure was marked by moments of achievement, but political gridlock (especially after 2010, when the Republicans regained control of Congress) and Obama's measured, pragmatic approach prevented him from implementing a full breadth of progressive policies. His speeches could rouse and inspire the electorate with their sweeping rhetoric and appeals to the American conscience, but turning those words into tangible results remained a challenge.

President Obama made U.S. history with his nomination and win in the 2008 presidential election. Pictured here, President Obama takes his oath at his inauguration with his wife, Michelle, by his side.

Still, there were many noteworthy accomplishments throughout Obama's presidency. In his first term, he staved off a severe economic crisis with a stimulus package that invested in infrastructure, renewable energy, education, and other public sectors. His signature achievement, the Affordable Care Act (sometimes called "Obamacare"), was signed into law in 2010. While it did not create a fully public, universal health-care system, it helped make health care more equitable overall. Among other things, it allowed more people access to subsidized health care, stipulated essential benefits that all insurers must provide, and prevented insurers from declining coverage to people with "pre-existing conditions"—chronic illnesses that may be expensive to treat.

Obama's achievements on the international front were mixed. He ended combat operations in Iraq and Afghanistan, though the United States retained a military presence in both countries that continues in 2018. He oversaw implementation of a nuclear deal with Iran and entered the United States into the Paris Agreement to combat climate change. (President Donald Trump withdrew from both in 2018, saying that they did not protect U.S. interests.) Obama's use of executive power to authorize drone strikes, **extrajudicial** killings (assassinations of people by governments without due legal process), and deportations of undocumented immigrants remain troubling aspects of his legacy.

The 2016 Election

In 2008, George W. Bush authorized $700 billion of taxpayer money in direct aid to the banks that had caused the financial crisis, some of which went to salary bonuses for executives. Trillions more were loaned in secret. Bush's decision would create dissent within both parties. On the right, the Republican-affiliated Tea Party movement began protesting excessive government spending around 2009; on the left, the Occupy Wall Street movement launched protests that drew attention to increasing economic inequality in 2011.

Since many of the activities that caused the crisis, such as insider trading, were fraudulent and possibly criminal, Obama's decision not to prosecute any of the bank executives involved was seen by some as capitulation to Wall Street. This was not helped by the fact that Obama backed the bailout as a senator in 2008. Voters from both parties began to feel like the needs of the economic

As "Operation Neptune's Spear"—the mission against Osama bin Laden—was underway, President Obama and the national security team were briefed, in real time, in the White House's Situation Room.

elite were being put above their own. A growing distrust in big business and the government's ability to regulate it paved the way for one of the most surprising elections in U.S. history.

The favored Democratic candidate was Hilary Clinton. She had served as Obama's secretary of state and had already mounted a presidential campaign of her own in 2008. Shortly after she announced her candidacy in 2015, however, a 74-year-old senator from Vermont named Bernie Sanders entered the primary race. Sanders was an independent, meaning he was not affiliated with either of the two main political parties. The race became more competitive than anyone had thought. Sanders built up a strong network of grassroots support, raising the bulk of his funds through small individual donations. His platform, which included things like universal health care, free college tuition, and a $15 minimum wage, was very popular among the progressive wing of the party, in contrast to Clinton's more centrist approach.

Though Sanders notched several victories in state primaries, Clinton ultimately secured the nomination. She ran against Republican nominee Donald Trump—a real-estate developer and reality-television star with no previous political experience—in 2016. In a stunning upset, Trump triumphed over Clinton that November. Reasons for her loss continue to be debated by the Democratic Party: some Democrats say that her policies did not offer enough to working-class Americans, while others believe Trump's victory was due to nativist, **misogynist**, or anti-immigrant sentiment.

Epilogue: Into the Future

The Democratic Party is currently at a crossroads. The more progressive, leftward flank advocates for robust public policy such as universal health care, while the traditionalist wing trusts more in bipartisan compromise, gradual reform, and market-based solutions to problems. The rise of groups such as the Democratic Socialists of America (DSA) and the victories of DSA-endorsed candidates in elections across the country have begun to push the party in a more leftward direction, with a groundswell of support for such programs as Medicare for All. In 2018, party leaders made a concession to progressives when they removed special privileges for superdelegates—representatives to party conventions who were seen as having too much power and influence over the nomination process. How all of this will impact the direction of the party over the next generation remains to be seen. At the very least, the fact that members are willing to stake out, debate, and defend positions shows they are committed to advancing the party.

Text-Dependent Questions

1. How did Republican candidate Richard Nixon use the chaos of the 1968 Democratic Convention to help him electorally?

2. Name one notable challenge that Jimmy Carter faced during his administration.

3. What was one element of Bernie Sanders's platform in 2016?

Research Project

Research the coverage of the 2016 Democratic primaries or 2016 general election from a variety of news sources. Compare and contrast writers' opinions of the candidates, points of criticism and support, and reasons given for victories and defeats. Write a summary of your findings, including how different sources choose to emphasize different things about candidates and their platforms.

Delegates celebrate at the 1992 Democratic Convention in Madison Square Garden, New York City.

Series Glossary of Key Terms

Abolitionist: A person committed to abolishing a certain practice, such as slavery or unfair criminal justice practices.

Acquittal: When a person is cleared of a charge of an offense.

Ambassador: A person who acts as the representative of a nation, organization, or other group in discussions or negotiations with others.

Amnesty: To give an official pardon to a person accused of an offense.

Appeal: In legal terms, to apply to a higher court to review, and possibly overturn, the decision of a lower court.

Apportionment: The division of something, such as money, among a group.

Bicameral: Used to describe a legislative body with two chambers.

Bond: A type of financial instrument in which the issuer agrees to repay an investor a certain amount of money with interest over time.

Cabinet: In government, a group of advisers of a head of state.

Canvass: To appeal directly to people in hopes of securing their votes.

Casework: Assistance in matters of government provided by a senator to a constituent, including answering questions, explaining policies, or determining eligibility.

Caucus: A gathering of members of a specific political party or organization to form policy positions, choose leaders, and make other decisions relevant to the organization.

Censure: To formally and publicly express disapproval of a person or action.

Census: An official count of a population, often including other data or information about that population.

Centrist: A politician who favors policies that are neither too liberal nor too conservative.

Chief justice: The highest ranking judge on a court with multiple judges; in the United States, the head of the Supreme Court.

Civil service: The professional public sector of a government (not including the military, judicial branches, or elected officials), staffed by people who are hired for their skills rather than elected or appointed.

Cloture: A means of ending debate on a bill in order to force a vote.

Common law: Laws based on past custom, or what has been judged over time to be lawful or unlawful.

Conference committee: In the U.S. Congress, a temporary committee made up of both House and Senate members, organized to prepare a version of an act that incorporates amendments from both chambers.

Constituent: A person who can vote and is represented by a public official.

Decentralized: Used to describe a system in which power is dispersed among people, states, or other entities, rather than controlled by one administrative body.

Deficit spending: When a government spends money that it has borrowed rather than collected through taxes.

Delegate: A person dispatched to represent others at a conference, legislative session, or other official event.

Demographic: A specific part of a population.

Deposition: Testimony taken down in writing.

Diplomat: An official representative of one country to another.

Duty: A tax or fee placed on imported or exported goods.

Egalitarian: Of or related to the belief that humans are equal, especially with respect to social, political, and economic rights and privileges.

Electoral College: A body of representatives from each state, who formally vote to elect the president and vice president.

Excise tax: A tax on a specific good or activity, often included in the overall price.

Executive branch: The U.S. government entity that enforces laws, with the president at its head.

Extrajudicial: Describing an act that is not legally authorized.

Federal deficit: The amount of money the federal government spends in excess of what it collects in taxes.

Federalist: An advocate of a central national government that unites states and leaves various powers to state governments.

Filibuster: The strategy of legislators talking indefinitely to prevent a vote on a bill.

Franchise: An individual's right to vote.

Gold standard: A monetary system where the value of currency is based on a specific quantity of gold.

Habeas corpus: A legal means by which a person can contest unlawful imprisonment; the term is Latin for "You have the body."

Impeachment: A charge of wrongdoing or misconduct against a public official that may result in termination from office.

Inaugurate: To begin a policy or practice; to formally admit someone into a public office.

Incumbent: A person currently holding a political office.

Indict: To formally charge someone of a crime.

Isolationist: A policy that favors limited or no engagement in international affairs.

Legislature: The assembly of a government or state that is tasked with making laws.

Libertarian: A person who believes completely in the free will and choice of individuals.

Line-item veto: The power of a chief executive to reject certain parts of a bill.

Lobbyist: A person who advocates for particular policies or positions.

Mandate: An instruction to do something in a certain way.

Motion: A formal proposal or request put before a legislative body.

Naturalization: The process of granting a person from one country citizenship of another country.

Originalism: When referring to the U.S. Constitution, a belief that the document should be interpreted along the lines of the Framers' original intent.

Pardon: To release someone of all punishments for a crime.

Parliamentarian: A person who advises a legislative body on matters of procedure.

Partisanship: Strong adherence to a particular cause or group, often at the expense of compromise with others.

Perjury: An act of lying under oath.

Platform: A set of policy goals on which a candidate bases a campaign.

Pocket veto: When a president indirectly vetoes a bill by leaving it unsigned as a legislative session expires.

Political action committee: An organization that raises funds to influence elections, ballot measures, or other legislation.

Polling: In politics, soliciting the opinions of the public to help determine electoral preferences.

Primary: An election within a political party to choose its candidates for a race.

Progressive: In political science, a person who seeks to advance society through implementation of new policies and ideas.

Pro tempore: A Latin phrase meaning "for the time being," used to describe when a person holds a position in the absence of a superior.

Provision: A requirement, restriction, or condition set forth in a legal document.

Quorum: The minimum number of members of a group who need to be present in order to officially conduct business.

Recession: A period of economic decline, with drops in both trade and production of goods.

Reprieve: To grant a delay in sentencing for a crime.

Resolution: A formal proposal adopted by a governing body.

Secession: The formal withdrawal from a state, alliance, or other political body.

Slip law: A document containing the complete text of a new law along with its legislative history, often the law's first published form.

Subpoena: A formal document ordering someone to provide evidence or testimony, most often to a court.

Subsidized: Funded by an outside source.

Suffragist: A person who advocates for others' right to vote.

Supermajority: A vote total that represents significantly more than one-half of the voting assembly, often 60 percent or two-thirds.

Tariff: A tax on imported or exported goods.

Treason: An act of betraying one's country.

Veto: The power to reject a legislative bill and refuse to sign it into law.

Original autographed ticket to the 1996 Democratic Convention held at the United Center in Chicago, Illinois. The convention nominated Bill Clinton and Al Gore for their second term as president and vice president of the United States.

Further Reading & Internet Resources

BOOKS

Friends Divided: John Adams and Thomas Jefferson. By Gordon S. Wood. Published in 2017 by Penguin Press, New York. Professor Gordon S. Wood examines the multifaceted relationship between John Adams and Thomas Jefferson as they worked together—and often disagreed—to create a republic.

Andrew Jackson and the Rise of the Democratic Party. By Mark R. Cheathem. Published in 2018 by the University of Tennessee Press, Knoxville, Tennessee. This book examines the factors that allowed Jackson's particular brand of populism to take hold in America.

No Ordinary Time: Franklin and Eleanor Roosevelt: The Home Front in World War II. By Doris Kearns Goodwin. Published in 1995 by Simon & Schuster, New York. Though there have been more recent studies of Franklin Roosevelt and his times, this Pulitzer Prize–winning book has been lauded for its intimate portrait of Roosevelt during the turbulent years of World War II, including the ways his wife, Eleanor, helped steer the ship of state.

Robert Kennedy and His Times: 40th Anniversary Edition. By Arthur Schlesinger Jr. Renowned historian and Kennedy confidante Arthur Schlesinger Jr. gives a portrait of Robert Kennedy and the tumultuous sixties, including the forces that shaped his political views and concern for the poor and marginalized.

Hacks. By Donna Brazile. Published in 2017 by Hachette Books, New York. The former chair of the Democratic National Committee tells an inside story of the 2016 election and how foreign interference might have influenced the outcome.

WEB SITES

The Democratic Party. http://www.democrats.org. The official site of the Democratic Party, featuring news and information about the party's platform.

Monticello: The Home of Thomas Jefferson. http://www.monticello.org. Learn more about Monticello, the Virginia home of Thomas Jefferson, at this official site.

**U.S. Presidents: An Online Reference Resource. https://millercenter.org/
president.** The Miller Center of Public Affairs at the University of Virginia
offers a trove of information about every U.S. president, including facts, photos,
and in-depth essays.

The Inaugural Addresses of the Presidents. http://avalon.law.yale.edu/subject_
menus/inaug.asp. The Avalon Project at Yale University maintains a digital
archive of documents related to law, economics, diplomacy, and government,
including this library of presidential inaugural addresses.

*John F. Kennedy, a Democrat, served as President of the United States from January
1961 until his assassination in November 1963.*

Index

Credits

COVER

(clockwise from top left) Pete Souza/Wikimedia Commons; Elias Goldensky/Library of Congress; Joseph Sohm/Shutterstock

INTERIOR

1, Joe Sohm/Dreamstime; 11, Everett Art/Shutterstock; 12, traveler1116/iStock; 14, John Trumbull/Wikimedia Commons; 17, Everett Historical/Shutterstock; 18, ivan-96/iStock; 19, J. Mund/Wikimedia; 21, Rembrandt Peale/Wikimedia; 24, Everett Historical/Shutterstock; 27, mashuk/iStock; 29, Everett Historical/Shutterstock; 31, White House History/Wikimedia Commons; 35, Everett Historical/Shutterstock; 36, Everett Historical/Shutterstock; 37, Everett Historical/Shutterstock; 40, Everett Historical/Shutterstock; 41, Everett Historical/Shutterstock; 45, Everett Historical/Shutterstock; 46, Everett Historical/Shutterstock; 51, Everett Historical/Shutterstock; 52, Everett Historical/Shutterstock; 55, Nathaniel Currier Firm/Wikimedia Commons; 58, Everett Historical/Shutterstock; 59, Everett Historical/Shutterstock; 63, Everett Historical/Shutterstock; 64, Library of Congress; 65, Everett Historical/Shutterstock; 67, Everett Historical/Shutterstock; 70, Everett Historical/Shutterstock; 73, Architect of the Capitol/Wikimedia Commons; 74 (UP), New York World-Telegram and the Sun Newspaper/Wikimedia Commons; 74 (LO), Harris & Ewing/Wikimedia Commons; 78, U.S. National Archives and Records Administration/Wikimedia Commons; 81, United Press International/Wikimedia Commons; 82, Walt Cisco, Dallas Morning News/Wikimedia Commons; 85, Arnold Newman, White House Press Office/Wikimedia Commons; 86, Cecil W. Stoughton/Wikimedia Commons; 88, UPI Photo Service/Newscom; 91, Department of Defense, Department of the Navy, Naval Photographic Center/Wikimedia Commons; 93, Warren K. Leffler/Wikimedia Commons; 95, Joseph Sohm/Shutterstock; 99, Master Sgt. Cecilio Ricardo, U.S. Air Force/Wikimedia; 101, Everett Collection/Newscom